Into Hostile Skies

Paul Novak

DEDICATION

This work is dedicated to Captain Richard Purinton, USAF, my friend and B52 aircraft commander, whose flying skill saved my life in the hostile skies of North Vietnam. Dick was diagnosed with leukemia shortly after the 1972 Christmas bombings. He died in 1974. He was a true hero.

~

It is also dedicated to the Wild Weasels—F-100, F-105, and F-4 crews—those who played their deadly game of hunt and kill suppressing the SA-2 missile sites—the deadliest of threats to the B-52s. And to the courageous F-4 pilots who flew Mig CAP protecting the Linebacker II BUFFs from the enemy's fighter aircraft. Finally, a salute to the heroic men and women who served in support of Linebacker II and to the brave pilots and crewmembers of the FB-111, KC-135, EB-66, EA-6, EA-3, F-111, U-2, SR-71, reconnaissance, and search and rescue aircraft who prepared the way, guarded the BUFFS, and ensured a successful result.

ACKNOWLEDGEMENTS

Writing a piece of history is difficult but would be impossible without documentation and references that provide accurate and knowledgeable data about the event. So it is with *Over the Fence*.

I would like to thank Brig. General James R. McCarthy (ret.) and Lt. Col. George B. Allison (ret.) for their brilliant and exhaustive study of the activities of that 11-day Christmas, 1972 operation, *Linebacker II, A View from the Rock*, upon which some of this piece is based. Their top-down perspective from the command and management view is a complement to my own story from the crew perspective, specifically about that flight on December 26th, 1972 into hostile skies over Hanoi, North Vietnam.

∞

My thanks to Lt. Col. Myles McTernan, USAF ret., Lt. Col. Jerry Wickline, USAF ret., and Lt. Col. Bill Milcarek, USAF ret., for their courageous service to our country. These men, the central figures in the *Last Man Out* story—navigator, command pilot, and co-pilot respectively—have generously assisted me with their story. Support without which such an amazing tale could not be told.

∞

For his dedicated service and bravery, and for his unparalleled assistance in digging out facts, photos, and personal memories so that *Nonstop Around the World* could come together, my sincere appreciation to Major Wayne Hesser, USAF ret., the lead radar-navigator on the B-52 crew that crossed Gaddafi's line of death in 1980.

∞

My gratitude to Major Wayne Goodson, Director of Information, Eighth Air Force, and to SMSgt John Sbrega, Editor, for **"The Mighty Eighth,** *A Report on SAC in Southeast Asia,* upon which our Bonus Feature, SAC in SE Asia, is based.

My eBooks

Mrs. President

Over the Fence

101+ Uncommonly Good Insights for Teens

Footprints After the Snow (Coming Jan. 2014)

Mrs. President II – The Omega Sanction

(Coming April 2014)

My Paperback Books

Mrs. President

Into Hostile Skies Anthology

Over the Fence

Last Man Out

Nonstop Around the World

B-52...History, Icon, Legend

Footprints After the Snow (Coming Jan. 2014)

Mrs. President II – The Omega Sanction

(Coming April 2014)

Coming Soon in Paperback and eBook...

*Read the Prologue to **Mrs. President II—The Omega Sanction** in this book after the final page of Into Hostile Skies. . .*

Table of Contents

Introduction to the Into Hostile Skies Anthology

When the B-52 Stratofortress was born in 1952 (first flight), Social Security full retirement age was pegged at 66 years for humans. And one would have stood aghast if anyone at its official rollout at Boeing Aircraft even suggested that the aircraft would be flying well past that age.

Well, don't look now, but the B-52 turns 66 in 2018, and the U.S. Air Force, as this story is written in 2013, has just initiated a massive, fleet wide $1.1 billion technological upgrade of this incredible, venerable, first-line U.S. strategic bomber. The Air Force emphasizes that a structural, service life, or air frame modification is not necessary and won't be until around 2040…on the H model's…wait for it…78th birthday.

This author was born five years before the B-52's first flight and flew as a navigator and radar-navigator/bombardier in the BUFF (Big Ugly Friendly Fellow) during the Vietnam War in the early 1970's. In all likelihood I won't be around to see its retirement. Now, that's a long history for an airplane.

This anthology of stories is my salute to my aircraft and to the most common denominator of all—the people who crewed her, both in the air and on the ground. The compilation herein consists of four tales: *Over the Fence*, *Last Man Out*, *Non-stop Around the World*, and *B-52…History, Icon, Legend!*

Over the Fence is three stories. It is the story of my Westover AFB crew's combat flight into the hostile skies over North Vietnam during the early 1970s. It was this eleven days of bombing over Christmas of 1972 that turned an aircraft which was already the symbol of the U.S. Cold War nuclear deterrent, into the symbol of U.S. power, fortitude, and endurance.

This is also the story of the command and management of this historical endeavor from the perspective of a couple gentlemen who know it best. My hat is off to them for their depiction of this angle of the Christmas bombings in their own document, "Linebacker II, a View from the Rock." You will find their names as I credit them with their contribution in the Acknowledgements of "Over the Fence."

And it is, perhaps most of all, a story of the people—the team—that made Linebacker II a success. You will read of the tremendous team effort and supreme sacrifice it took to bring the enemy back to the negotiating table and to free the U.S. prisoners-of-war in Hanoi and elsewhere. In the same story you will have an inside look at a professional, poised B-52 combat crew—mine—as we prepared for and executed this mission while facing an onslaught of surface-to-air missiles (SAMs). And perhaps you will be surprised by the turn this story takes at its ending.

Last Man Out is the story of a friend of mine and his crew. "Mush" as we knew him then was a fellow-instructor at the Navigator-Bombardier Training Squadron at Mather AFB, California. We met there in 1975, after both of our stories had been lived and survived.

Myles McTernan was also a navigator aboard a B-52 during the 11-day Christmas bombing of North Vietnam. Not as fortunate as I, his aircraft took a direct hit from a SAM while flying a post-Christmas mission over Vinh, and the crew was forced to bail out over open ocean. I'll let the story itself tell the rest, but you will be enthralled, I think, by the courage of this crew and by Myles's perseverance in hostile skies and seas, and his will to survive.

Nonstop Around the World*, Crossing Gaddafi's Line of Death,* is the narrative of two elite crews from K.I. Sawyer Air Force Base in Michigan and their difficult, harrowing, non-stop, around-the-world journey. Told from the perspective of former Capt. Wayne

Hesser, Radar-navigator aboard the lead aircraft, the story will hold your attention and surprise you with the descriptions of the dangers and difficulties they faced, including crossing Muammar Gaddafi's "line of death," and photographing the Soviet Navy in an era that was dominated by the Cold War. It will also thrill the patriotic side of you as you read of their rendezvous with and low-level flyover of the U.S.S. Nimitz aircraft carrier halfway around the globe in the Arabian Gulf.

B-52...History, Icon, Legend is the story of the aircraft itself. Incomplete as it must be, it will give you a summary view of the extensive multiple roles it has played so far in this country's military history. It has seen service from the opening of the Cold War period, through airborne nuclear alert, Vietnam, Iraq in Operation Desert Storm, the Balkan wars, Afghanistan, and a second time over Iraq, up to the present day. And its missions and capabilities have changed and improved with each decade as it has become a flying platform for the latest aviation and warfare technology.

We will look at the future of the aircraft and see how favorably it compares to its modern-day peers, the B-1 and B-2. In doing so, we will see why it has been and will remain this nation's primary frontline bomber for decades to come.

There are so many of these stories, and many thousands of current and former B-52 crewmembers who claim the aircraft as I do—"mine." It is because, despite the danger, despite the age of the aircraft, and despite the rigors of the life of a combat crewmember aboard the B-52, it was and is a time to be cherished, remembered, and claimed by those who participated. We are proud that we have been part of the most effective, endurable, and history-making jet aircraft in the past, present, and future of this country's military flight history...

...and we all know that there will never, ever be another like her.

Over the Fence

Preamble

"When the 11 days of LINEBACKER II are viewed as a whole, one of the notable achievements was the ability of the flight crews to be able to fly these complex tactics in combat, in mass formations, without benefit of practice.

"In my opinion, this will eventually be recognized as one of the most outstanding feats of airmanship in strategic bombing operations in the history of aerial warfare."

Brigadier General James R. McCarthy (ret.),
Wing Commander, 43rd Strategic Wing, Andersen AFB
Airborne Mission Commander, 26 December 1972

Back story

From December 18 to December 29, 1972, Strategic Air Command B-52s, this nation's frontline bomber, flew 729 sorties against 34 targets in North Vietnam. They expended over 15,000 tons of ordnance in the process. Bomb damage assessment revealed 1,600 military structures damaged or destroyed, 500 railroad interdictions, 372 pieces of rolling stock damaged or destroyed, and three million gallons of petroleum products destroyed (estimated to be one-fourth of North Vietnam's reserves). Numerous airfields, runways, and ramps were damaged or destroyed, and an estimated 80 per cent of electrical power production capability eliminated.

This level of damage was astounding considering the fact that many had believed the B-52s would be decimated by the defenses of the most heavily defended city in the world at the time, as described by Walter Boyne in the November 1997 issue of Air Force Magazine:

"In 1965, that enemy heartland had been virtually defenseless and could have been attacked at will. Now, (in 1972) after a huge buildup, it was shielded by the most extensive and strongest integrated air defense system in the world.

"The size and strength of those defenses were so great that many believed the B-52 heavy bomber, backbone of the Air Force's long-range force, would not be able to survive encounters with it.

"By 1972, North Vietnam had amassed a defense that included 145 Mig fighters, 26 SA-2 Guideline surface-to-air missile sites (21 in the Hanoi-Haiphong area), a heavy concentration of anti-aircraft artillery, and a complex, overlapping radar network that served an efficient and many-times-redundant command-and-control system. In addition, the radar network secretly had been improved in recent times by introduction of a new fire-control radar that improved the accuracy of the SA-2 weapons."[1]

There is no way to estimate the enormous amount of AAA, or the amount of cannon and rocket ordnance used by the North Vietnamese Mig fighters against the B-52s. The only stated figure indicative of the defensive reaction is a best estimate on total surface-to-air missiles fired at B-52s by the SAM sites. One guess is 884. (Another source suggests as many as 1,242; another estimates 914.) The more amazing figure is that of the conservative figure of 884, only twenty-four achieved hits, for a 2.7 percent

---

Walter J. Boyne, *"Linebacker II"*, Air Force Magazine (November, 1997) **http://www.afa.org/magazine/Nov1997/1197lineback.html**

success rate of launches to hits. Of the twenty-four, fifteen resulted in a downed aircraft. That equates to a 1.7 percent kill rate for the number of SAMs launched.

There were ninety-two crewmembers aboard the fifteen downed aircraft. Fourteen are known or declared killed-in-action (KIA). Fourteen remain missing-in-action. (These two numbers have changed over the years, and remain approximate). Thirty-three who became POWs survived and were subsequently repatriated.

Close Call

"Damn," yelled 'Mac' McNeil, our co-pilot, twenty minutes from the target southeast of Hanoi. "That thing came up right between 6 and 7. Should've blown up."[2]

"That thing" meant a North Vietnamese SA-2 surface-to-air missile (SAM) should have destroyed the right wing of our B-52 but didn't detonate. I tightened the straps holding me into my ejection seat.

No Reply

U.S. B52s, along with additional Navy and Air Force aircraft, had hammered North Vietnam for a week prior to Christmas Eve, 1972. Then, President Nixon ordered a stand-down on Christmas Day. He sent a message to the North Vietnamese and offered to halt the bombing if they returned to the peace negotiations. When there was no reply from North Vietnam, the President ordered the resumption of the bomb raids.

On December 26th, 1972, U.S. military aircraft thundered into Hanoi and Haiphong with the largest massed air attack of B52s in the history of aerial warfare. One hundred twenty of this country's strategic bombers struck at the heart of North Vietnam under cover of night. Within 15 minutes, all seven waves of bombers dropped a total of six million pounds of explosives on the capital city of Hanoi, and North Vietnam's major port, Haiphong. Over 700 flight

---

[2] The B-52 has 4 engine nacelles with 2 engines on each nacelle. The engines are numbered from 1 to 8 starting with the farthest engine from the aircraft on the pilot's side. #6 and #7 would be the second and third engines from the aircraft on the co-pilot's side. The missile came within 50 feet of the aircraft.

crewmembers went through a living-hell that night to complete that mission. Some did not come back.

My Story

I was the navigator of one of those B-52s and this is the story of my Westover AFB crew's flight from Andersen AFB into those hostile skies over Hanoi, North Vietnam, and of the events leading up to it during the operation called LINEBACKER II.

I am sometimes asked about the name "LINEBACKER." As we heard the rumor later, the origin of the "code" name was not some mysterious combination of secret words or phrases issued by the Joint Chiefs or the CIA to identify the mission. As far as we know, President Nixon suggested it because he was a football fan. Given the duties and characteristics of the linebacker function in that game, he thought it appropriate for this application. Besides, there had been a LINEBACKER I bombing operation in the southern part of North Vietnam, so I guess this was a natural follow-on designator for the Christmas bombings.

*

Some preliminaries are important, I think, to give the reader a sense of the enormous complexities of planning and executing such a mission. There were problems involved and dealt with, decisions that had to be made—some from minute-to-minute as the mission progressed—and a massive involvement and co-ordination of people in dozens of locations that had to work as a team to get our crews off the ground and the bombs on target.

I have also included some details about my personal life and family in the weeks before the Christmas bombings because I think they tend to give human perspective to this story. After all is said and done, this dangerous mission was my job. And as with all the other crews who fought by my side in Vietnam, my personal life, my family, and my country will always come first

Our purpose during the LINEBACKER II operation—those eleven days and nights of Christmas, 1972—was to bring North Vietnam to its knees so that we could end the U.S. involvement in Vietnam, and bring our prisoners-of-war home.

Did we succeed? Many argue both sides of that question.

As Dr. Henry Kissinger commented on January 24, 1973:

"...there was a deadlock...in the middle of December (1972), and there was a rapid movement when negotiations (with the North Vietnamese) resumed on January 8th. These facts have to be analyzed by each person for himself."[3]

It is fact that three days after that diplomatically worded response, an agreed-upon ceasefire went into effect.

It is also fact that on February 12, 1973 a C-141A Starlifter transport jet lifted off from Hanoi, North Vietnam, and the first of several flights of U.S. prisoners of war began its journey home.

Setting the Scene

Until early 1972 all B-52 bombing missions into Vietnam were launched from U-Tapao Royal Thai Navy Airfield located in the southwest corner of Thailand. The program was identified as ARC LIGHT and individual sorties flown supported American ground operations in South Vietnam.

The B-52s actually flew close-in air support for several major ground operations in South Vietnam during the late 1960s. According to the U.S. command structure the bombers were quite effective in terrorizing the Viet Cong fighting there. An account of the after-effects of a B-52 attack follows:

"Those entering a typical B-52 target area found the landscape torn as if by an angry giant. The bombs uprooted trees and scattered them in crazy angles over the ground. The tangled jungle undergrowth was swept aside around the bomb craters, sometimes revealing previously hidden field fortifications and openings to tunnel systems. The holes blasted in the jungle canopy made convenient landing zones for helicopters supporting the advance of the infantry. Upon occasion caches of enemy materiel (rice, salt, clothing, ammunition, weapons, medical supplies, and documents)

---

[3] Henry A. Kissinger, News Conference on 24 January 1973.
Quote from *Linebacker II, A View from the Rock*, USAF Southeast Asia Monograph Series, Volume VI, Monograph 8,
Office of Air Force History, Washington D.C., 1985. (See Acknowledgements)

were located and either confiscated or destroyed. Only rarely was any enemy dead found, although reports often spoke of trails of blood, used bandages, and a "smell of death" which lingered in the area. The Viet Cong were usually quite thorough in carrying off their wounded and dead or burying them in the interval between the end of the bombing and the arrival of troops."[4]

TDY

Crews from all B-52 bomb wings in the U.S. were called upon to serve 120-180 day temporary duty tours (TDY) at U-Tapao to support this operation. The crews were sent TDY and then rotated home so that they could be sent again if needed. Most B52D crews I knew served from 3-5 of those TDY tours either at U-Tapao or Andersen AFB, Guam.

In parallel with the U-Tapao operation ARC LIGHT, B-52Ds were also being maintained on nuclear alert at Andersen AFB— almost 3000 miles away. The 43rd Strategic Bomb Wing there also held responsibility for a back-up war plan to supplement bombing missions out of U-Tapao into Vietnam if and when needed. What no one realized in early 1972 was how soon and to what an enormous scale that support would be needed, and how much LINEBACKER II would stretch the capabilities of Andersen AFB to handle the crews, support personnel and equipment, and aircraft.

The Build-up

Things began to change in early February, 1972 when many crews in the U.S. were called to pack their bags, hug their families, and be ready to go overseas in only a few hours. They would board a KC-135 along with crews from other SAC bases for the long trip, or ferry a B-52 over the pond to Guam or Thailand because aircraft were needed too. All of this activity came to be known as BULLET SHOT—a planned, methodical buildup of B-52 and support personnel needed to choke off the increased penetration of the North Vietnamese and Vietcong guerilla forces into South Vietnam. And those gas-loving BUFFS consumed a lot of fuel

---

[4] Robert M. Kipp, *Counterinsurgency From 30,000 Feet, The B-52 in Vietnam*, Air University Review, January-February 1968

on the 12-hour flights to and from Vietnam. They needed to be refueled in-flight which required a parallel buildup of KC-135 tankers and their flight crews at Kadena Air Base on the island of Okinawa and elsewhere. There was no room at Andersen which exploded from 4,000 personnel to 12,000 in residence by July, 1972 brought about by an additional 100 B-52Gs and their crews, along with an expanded B-52D force of 50 airplanes, crews, support personnel, support equipment, etc.

Permanent billets were not available for all those personnel so tent cities went up around the base to house them in less than adequate surroundings. And tin buildings made of corrugated sheeting left over from a bygone era built to temporarily hold 80 people became overloaded with 175 people or more.

Our crew was one of the extremely lucky ones. Though Dick Purinton and I lived off-base with our families during this TDY, on subsequent TDYs, and while the build-up was still present in case something went wrong with the peace process, all six of us were housed in two attached permanent dormitory rooms that usually slept two. But it was pure luxury as we walked out on our balcony and looked down on the poor guys housed in one of the tent cities right below us. I used to wonder what the opposite view looked like and what they might be thinking about our "hotel" vs. their "canvas camp." I don't think I would have wanted to eavesdrop on their comments.

Same Aircraft, Different Models

Both the B-52G and B-52D model aircraft flew the missions of LINEBACKER II from Andersen and U-Tapao. At Andersen, the G model outnumbered the Ds 2:1. Approximately 100 Gs and 50 Ds presented some hurdles for aircrew training and maintenance since they were different aircraft and the systems onboard took some familiarization to work with.

The other complicating problem was that crews from B-52G or H model bases in the states might have to fly B-52D aircraft in LINEBACKER II. The B-52D could carry more bombs and had better defensive countermeasures at the time. So the crews required transition training both in the States and at Andersen to accomplish that changeover from one aircraft type to another. The final step of that training was to fly up to three actual combat missions with a more experienced pilot upstairs in the jump seat and senior radar navigator monitoring downstairs.

The B-52G had more powerful engines than the B-52D. This presented the pilot with a problem in transitioning from one aircraft to the other in that the D model seemed "underpowered" to a G-model pilot. Air refueling became the point where those differences showed up most significantly due to the "finesse" required to nudge the BUFF up to the tanker refueling nozzle in order for the airplane to get a much needed drink.

And, downstairs, for the navigators, the equipment was positioned differently and some of the radar equipment put out different levels of energy so the RN had to adjust his thinking regarding radar aiming points for the crucial bomb run. Since the navigator always assisted the RN with the target aim points, this became his hurdle too.

Defensively, the Electronic Warfare Officer (EWO) and the Gunner had their own conversion to master. The G model gunner sat in the forward crew compartment with the rest of the crew. The D model gunner sat in his own isolated compartment in the tail of the aircraft—a striking divergence. Fortunately, the equipment he operated in the tail was almost identical to what he had operated in the G model. The EW also operated similar equipment as he had in the G model. However, the switch locations were somewhat different. He had to keep his head in the display scope and feel for the switches during a combat mission, so it was vital to airplane and crew safety that he made sure of the new locations of those control functions.

Back-breaking Bomb Loading

No piece about the Christmas bombings would be complete without a nod to and a description of the Bomb Loaders who kept the aircraft loaded with the weapons that made the long, dangerous trips over North Vietnam worthwhile at all.

To put it succinctly, those dedicated crews of young men loaded about 58,000 bombs, each weighing 500-750 pounds, into the B-52s' bellies and under their wings. And though satisfactory equipment was available and utilized, the last mind-bending, muscle-tearing, straining, sweat-filled few inches had to be conquered through sheer muscle power, frustration, and cussing. Take that times tens of thousands of weapons and you can get the feel for the magnitude of the task.

The other part of the difficulty was the time allowed to do it. Under normal conditions at Andersen and at U-Tapao, bomb loaders worked a 12-hour shift six days a week. During the 11-day bombings, it became seven-days a week, 24 hour job. And because of the sheer volume, personnel were pulled from other jobs to assist in the vital function.

There was preciseness about their work, though it became very much an assembly-line operation which, by definition, consisted of separate routine, repetitive mundane tasks. But the routine could not become one that did not result in 100 per cent operable weapons on every aircraft. The whole had to be greater than its parts. And with the dedicated men who performed this function, it was. They knew how important these weapons were and exactly where they were going. They felt as strongly as the flight crews did that they had an important part to play. There is no case I can recall that improper bomb loading caused a weapon not to be released. That's perfection.

Maintaining the Massive Fleet

We tend to think of LINEBACKER II in terms of the massive damage and havoc it rained on North Vietnam for 11 days of 1972, for the aircraft and crewmembers lost, for the historical tonnage of bombs released, and for the hundreds of SA-2 missiles fired at the B-52s which made it miraculous that as many escaped "over the fence" to fly again. And, of course, we know it as the precursor to bringing the POWs home.

But we don't give much thought to the awe-inspiring maintenance support that kept the 155 Andersen AFB B-52s flying, refueled them, repaired the battle damage, fixed immediate equipment failures before and after missions, and accomplished normal scheduled maintenance items in record times with minimal facilities and equipment.

The constricted time allowed between missions forced maintenance crews to slash the time allowed by 50-75% for normal maintenance items like refueling, bomb-loading, phase inspections, engine overhaul, tire changes, etc.

One example is the engine overhauls. In the U.S. a normal B-52 bomb wing might overhaul 5-10 engines a month. The number of aircraft at Andersen and the mission load necessitated over 100 overhauls a month.

Many of the maintenance troops lived in the worst of housing conditions on Andersen or were bused from off-base locations which could add two hours to their workday, already a minimum of 12 hours. Yet, as with the bomb loading, it was rare that any individual aircraft was not able to meet its assigned launch. And if that did happen, the maintenance and ground crews had pre-staged a "bag-drag" aircraft spare that the flight crew could transition to and complete the mission.

∞
December 26th, 1972 – Target Hanoi

The Briefing…and absolution
The main difference between this strike on the 26th and the bombings of the prior week was that all 78 primary B52 crews at Andersen AFB, Guam had to be briefed at the same time and would take off consecutively in one launch. The remaining 42 aircraft would launch from U-Tapao AB, Thailand, timed to coincide with the target times of the Andersen aircraft.

An emotional and unusual moment occurred during a massed Andersen briefing when the Roman Catholic priest who got the duty call for the pre-mission prayer, and who was well aware of the danger of this mission, sensed the pensive mood of the crews. In addition to his blessing and prayer, he apologized, then performed the extraordinary act of pronouncing absolution and benediction to those present. Circumstances would not allow for it later for those who would not return from the mission. It brought a silence to the crews unlike anything I had ever experienced in a mission briefing. I think it hammered home, in a gentle way, the totality and potential finality of the dangerous skies we were about to fly into.

The Launch

Thousands of observers noted what a spectacular sight it was to watch the massive, complex dance of the largest single launch of B52s ever undertaken—78 B52s choreographed into position from five miles of revetments and taxiways, and lined up for a take-off sequence which would last for two and a half hours. Within the big dance, each 3-ship cell had to be maneuvered so that they took off sequentially to alleviate problems coordinating once airborne. There were 26 3-ship cells.

It truly was, as Major Bill Stocker, in command of the lead aircraft said, "One of the most awesome armadas ever assembled."

Enemy Eyes on the Launch

The Russian ship that always monitored Andersen departures saw the launch too, and radioed North Vietnam that the B52s were coming. This would be no surprise attack, but the fact that 120 aircraft would converge over Hanoi and Haiphong from multiple directions within the same 15-minute timeframe would, hopefully, stretch the limits of the North Vietnamese defensive response.

As the crews would later find out, this wasn't necessarily always the case. Two B52s would be lost that night over Hanoi because of a significant increase in SAM launches. The North Vietnamese had restocked during the one-day Christmas stand-down of B52 strikes. And their SAM missile crews had a week of experience launching at B-52s with some success.

Air Refueling – The First Obstacle

Eight-engine B52s require a huge amount of fuel to accomplish a 15-hour mission from Guam to North Vietnam and back. Normally in a three-ship cell of BUFFs, this is not a problem. We meet a KC-135 tanker aircraft out of Kadena AB, Okinawa somewhere north of the Philippines and that's that. The same would have been true on this historic massed mission only on a much larger scale. All was planned well and ready to be executed, but no one could have predicted that a C-141 flying into Kadena with an emergency at exactly the wrong time would delay the KC-135 takeoffs by 15 minutes. This meant that all already-airborne 78 B52s from Andersen would arrive at their refueling control

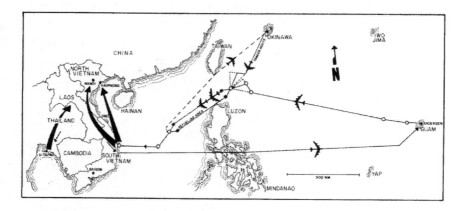

The B-52s flew these routes to and from Andersen AFB, Guam to South Vietnam, and from U-Tapao AB, Thailand, then dispersed into attack formation to strike North Vietnam. The KC-135 tankers would launch from Kadena AFB, Okinawa and meet the B-52s north of the Philippines to refuel them. [5]

points too far ahead of the tankers to allow a rendezvous. A total disaster in the making which could scrub the entire mission.

The entire refueling route had to be moved closer to Kadena with the B52s already in the air, instructions passed to all aircraft of the change, and, most important of all, it all had to be successfully accomplished by each crew. Myriad other problems created by this snafu had to be solved as well like staying on time to the targets, and joining up with the dozens of support aircraft that would participate in the raid and protect the bombers on their way to the target.

But accomplished it was, and with amazing timeliness and skill. All rendezvous were made, fuel transferred, routes adjusted so that

---

[5] McCarthy& Allison, Linebacker II, A View from the Rock, 1985, p.4

target timing could be maintained, support aircraft met so the B52s were protected, and the bombing mission accomplished—on time.

One can understand why General McCarthy said what he did as quoted in the Prologue to this story. The complexity, sophistication, and professionalism necessary by all 78 crews to successfully complete the mission, even without all the added obstacles, had been awesome—(even if I do say so myself).

Bombs Away

Seventy-five of our heavy strategic bombers hit Hanoi while 45 attacked the port city of Haiphong. The B-52s came in all at the same time from Andersen and U-Tapao, and from multiple directions and altitudes, and hit all the targets in that 15-minute span in an unprecedented feat of aircraft coordination.

All seven waves of bombers dropped a total of 3,000 tons (6,000,000 pounds) of explosives on the two cities flying against a sky-filled night of Soviet-built surface-to-air missiles that traveled three times as fast as the B52. One B52 pilot said later that he felt he "could have walked across the sky on the tips of the missiles there were so damn many of them."

SAMs—The Second Problem

The North Vietnamese used three means of air defense around Hanoi and Haiphong. That fact, the use of Russian technology, and the sheer massed quantity of SAMs are the reasons Hanoi was considered the most heavily defended city in the world at the time the B-52s struck. The three threats were anti-aircraft fire, Russian Mig fighter jets, and hundreds of Russian SAMs.

Each B-52 had it own electronic countermeasures (ECM), and a dedicated Electronic Warfare Officer to operate them to full effect against incoming missiles. The bomber carried a pod of jammers that created an electronic cloud that radiated and covered the aircraft's specific location. Then, planners maximized this effect by always flying in cells of three aircraft. In a steep turn or a post-bomb drop turn, the countermeasures lost some of their affectivity. The North Vietnamese knew this and made every effort to take advantage of it. It was during this steeper post-target turn that several B-52s were lost.

The other support aircraft increased the effects of electronic countermeasures (ECM). Some of the F-4's equipped for ECM also laid down chaff corridors of metal strips to widen the "cloud."

The North Vietnamese used Spoon Rest early warning radar which had a range of about 170 miles and would initially spot the incoming aircraft. The Spoon Rest then handed off the target to a Fan Song fire control radar which directed the SA-2s. At about 40 miles out the Fan Song could then refine the location, altitude and speed of the incoming B-52s. However, any Fan Song that transmitted for too long became a target for American Wild Weasels, (described below).

Since AAA was effective only up to 20,000 feet, it proved useless against the B-52s. However, during the Vietnam War, it did seem to take its toll against lower flying fighter and bomber jets. But tactics developed by the Air Force and Navy did prove successful at avoiding the "walls of flak" that North Vietnamese gunners would throw up.

Combined Air Force and Navy aircraft guarded the B-52s as they made their combat attacks on the North Vietnamese cities.

Support aircraft usually included F-4s—either dropping chaff or armed as fighter aircraft, EB-66 electronics jamming aircraft, and the Wild Weasels, which were F-100, F105, or F-4 aircraft, that would bait enemy missile defenses into targeting them with their radars, then trace the radar beams back to the source, and target the source with an air-to-ground missile to destroy the entire SAM site. In addition, as the B-52s approached Hanoi, low-flying FB-111 fighter-bombers attacked North Vietnamese Mig airfields.

The Russian-built Mig 17s, 19s, and 21s, though every bit as technologically current as American fighters, did not figure into the U.S. strike plan as a major threat. Due to darkness, the attack altitude of the B-52s, and the combat air patrol of American fighters and surveillance aircraft, no one thought the Migs could account for any B-52 aircraft casualties on the U.S. side. However, they were launched against the massive bomber force to "pace" the aircraft and radio back altitude and speed to the SAM missile operations surrounding the two main cities. As mentioned elsewhere, two Migs were shot down by B-52 gunners during the 11-day campaign.

Darkness denied the North Vietnamese any potential for a visual SA-2 shoot down capability they may have hoped for against the B-52. But the SAM held its position as the number one threat against the B-52, and, after being pounded by B-52s in South Vietnam for years where they provided ground support for U.S. troops, the SAM batteries that permeated North Vietnam couldn't wait for a crack at a BUFF.

Each B-52 had it own electronic countermeasures (ECM), and a dedicated Electronic Warfare Officer to operate them to full effect against incoming missiles. The bomber carried a pod of jammers that created an electronic cloud that radiated and covered the aircraft's specific location. Then, planners maximized this effect by always flying in cells of three aircraft. In a steep turn or a post-bomb drop turn, the countermeasures lost some of their affectivity. The North Vietnamese knew this and made every effort to take advantage of it. It was during this steeper post-target turn that several B-52s were lost.

The other support aircraft increased the effects of electronic countermeasures (ECM). Some of the F-4's equipped for ECM also laid down chaff corridors of metal strips to widen the "cloud."

The North Vietnamese used Spoon Rest early warning radar which had a range of about 170 miles and would initially spot the incoming aircraft. The Spoon Rest then handed off the target to a Fan Song fire control radar which directed the SA-2s. At about 40 miles out the Fan Song could then refine the location, altitude, and speed of the incoming B-52s. However, any Fan Song that transmitted for too long became a target for American Wild Weasels, those U.S. aircraft described earlier that homed in on their transmissions.

As the B-52s approached Hanoi, North Vietnamese radars tracked the cloud and telephoned its position to the SA-2 battalions. The battalions often found the jamming too intense to use their own Spoon Rest radars to acquire a B-52 in the electronic smokescreen.

Ideally, the Fan Song fire control radar automatically tracked its target, but the American jamming usually made automatic tracking impossible. Instead, the North Vietnamese relied upon manual tracking, a difficult process that required the guidance operators to manually keep the target in the crosshairs.

The battalions' Fan Song fire control radars could only briefly discern the B-52s when they flew close by or when they made a post-bombing turn that reduced the B-52s ECM effectiveness and occasionally allowed for the Fan Song's more accurate automatic tracking mode to be used. This is when the ground crews fired most of their SA-2s.

∞

Flashback to the Personal

This day, December 26th, 1972, began with far less excitement.

There existed in my life at that time only one important thing-- the blissful time I spent with my wife and two young sons who had flown from Massachusetts to stay with me for a few months in Thailand and then Guam during my third TDY rotation to SE Asia. My pilot, Captain Dick Purinton had done the same and on this historic day our families now occupied two apartments in a modern building a few miles from Andersen AFB, Guam. And there are hundreds of other stories just like ours. This is but to give the reader a hint at the personal life of a combat flight crewmember.

After two previous lengthy combat deployments to the war in SE Asia, we had both decided that our families needed to be with us, and we needed it even more. So, in October, 1972, they flew from Massachusetts to Alaska to Hawaii to Guam to Bangkok, Thailand where we picked up two terribly exhausted and almost disoriented wives and the four little ones who had endured so much just to get close to Daddy. I don't think I ever appreciated enough the sacrifices those women made to do what they did. We took them to a nice, local Bangkok hotel where they collapsed into bed and slept for the next 12 hours. Their experience made my combat flights look like a walk in the park.

Bomb trains from B-52D aircraft on an Arc Light mission hitting suspected enemy troop positions in South Vietnam. (US Force photo)

B-52D (tall tail) dropping weapons over Vietnam. Note: Forward bombs are coming off the under-wing bomb racks. The B-52D holds 84 bombs internally and 24 under the wings. (USAF Photo)

SA-2 Missile similar to one used against B-52s during Linebacker II

B-52D Cockpit. Note extreme wear & tear on pilot's control yoke. This is from over 30 years of constant use in addition to hundreds of combat missions flown for each B-52D aircraft in Vietnam. (National Museum of the US Air Force Photo)

Dick Purinton – A/C(r)
Mac McNeil – CP
Ralph Testa – EW
R&R for crew at
beach – Andersen
1972

(Photo taken by
Paul Novak)

1st Lt. Paul Novak
Flight line – Andersen
1972

(Photo taken by
Dick Purinton)

B52D rear gunner's cockpit
Note: Back of seat folded down for entry
into rear Gunner's cockpit
Note: The entire aft portion of the
cockpit is jettisoned in order for the
Gunner to fall "forward" to bail out.

Bomb damage - Bac Mai Airfield, Hanoi, N. Vietnam
Note: B-52 bomb train pattern l to r edge of photo where
"runway interdicted" is labelled

The railroad network and spurs were vital to N. Vietnam's transport of
military goods. They were rendered useless

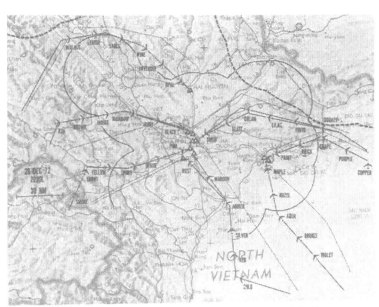

26 Dec 1972 10 Targets 40 3-ship cells of B-52s.
120 B-52s struck Hanoi and Haiphong within a 15-min. period

Note the multiple attack routes the B-52s flew into Hanoi and the fact
that this massive onslaught was conducted from every compass point
and all target times condensed to within 15 min.

After the losses——considered devastating——to the B-52s on the first
three nights caused by planning that brought the aircraft into Hanoi on
the same routes each night, mission design for 26 Dec was placed in the
capable hands of Eighth Air Force. This resulted in overpowering
the enemy's defenses and not allowing them time to "reload" their
surface-to-air missiles resulted in devastating damage levels to this key.
 railroad junction

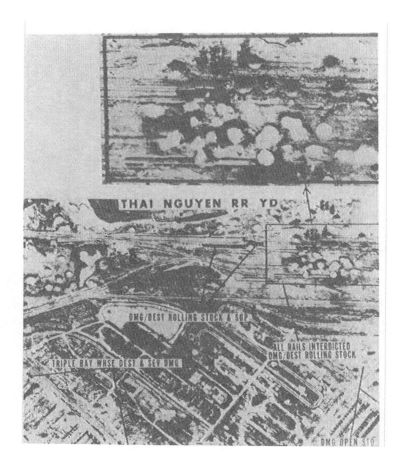

THAI NGUYEN RR YD

DMG/DEST ROLLING STOCK & SUP

ALL RAILS INTERDICTED
DMG/DEST ROLLING STOCK

TRIPLE BAY WHSE DEST & SEV DMG

DMG OPEN STO

Thai Nguyen Railroad Yard was a significant military and commercial crossroad in the enemy's transportation network. The inset (upper right) shows that the concentration and precision of the B-52 bombardment resulted in devastating damage levels to this key railroad junction

We stayed in Pattaya Beach, Thailand, a beach resort city located on the Gulf of Thailand about 15 miles north of our B52 base at U-Tapao, a Royal Thai Naval Air Base transformed to launch our aircraft on bomb runs into Vietnam. The wives located a very clean American compound of 2-story one-bedroom apartments where American doctors resided.

We obtained a Thai house girl, Noy, who became the center of our universe and the savior who did everything for us—babysit, clean, cook, shop for fresh Thai seafood at the local market, and kill a poisonous snake that crawled behind the stove one day while we were out. She charged the awesome fee of fifty cents a day for all this.

I remember to this day her sweet, smiling face and friendly personality as she sat cradling our youngest while she ate her meager lunch on our back porch with the other local house girls.

We ended up paying her far more than she asked and supplied her with cases of the much-desired peanut butter Thai people used in their recipes. Many of these tasty dishes she cooked for us and I remember the joy of devouring all of them. My eldest son, four years old at the time, ate the scrumptious Thai Jasmine rice like popcorn.

What a time and what a joy to have family and Noy to come home to after flying a combat mission over Vietnam. Surreal might be a good adjective to describe it. Noy and her sister house girls even helped us serve a Thai dinner for the rest of our crew who had not experienced their hospitality or their wonderful cooking skills and recipes.

I remembered that I had friends, drafted into the Vietnam War, who led a very different—bizarre one might claim—existence in the jungles of South Vietnam. Instead of family and a home-cooked meal and the safe protectorate of a country, they went home at night to a hovel in the jungle with a strand of barbed wire to protect them and a dismal existence I still can't fathom. Close quarter firefights with an enemy they couldn't see or hear, cold rations, and the stress of whether or not they might live through the next hour let alone ever get to see family again provided no solace at all.

Rotate to Guam

During the first week of December, 1972 our crew relocated to Andersen AFB, Guam as part of normal crew rotation. Dick Purinton and I moved our families into that modern apartment building which overlooked the South Pacific and the most awesome red, purple, yellow, and pink sunsets I have ever seen. Instead of 3-hour missions from Thailand to Vietnam, our marathons increased to 12 hours plus brief and debrief time. But we did fly less than the six days in a row we flew out of U-Tapao, so that we regarded as a plus. At this time, almost all B-52 missions headed for South Vietnam to support our ground troops there.

It soon became obvious that something momentous would take place and that the aircrews at Andersen would play a large role in it. Everything ramped up soon after we arrived and rumors that the B52s would invade North Vietnam seemed to go beyond the rumor stage when we looked around the Andersen AFB flight line and noted the increased level of organized chaos. (See our 3rd story).

Missed Call

B52 crews at Andersen, placed on standby 12-hour alert, roamed the island as always and that is what caused our command pilot, Dick Purinton, to miss the call to hightail it to the operations center briefing room on the 26th.

Anyone who has ever been part of a team or a crew that goes into a combat situation knows the vital necessity to have the team together. The sense of confidence, team cooperation, and shared risk elevate to the level of emotional necessity. To go with a substitute command pilot would be akin to the loss of motivation one might feel if the mission itself had to proceed into hostile territory without bombs in the bomb bay.

The vulnerability I felt, and that, I am certain, the rest of the crew suffered without Dick present at that briefing, preflight, and pre-taxi stage of the mass mission to bomb Hanoi, permeated our activities. The crew bus ride out to the aircraft became silent and lonely. No one said a word.

We sat in our positions, all the preflight activities accomplished, the bomb pins pulled, ready to taxi to our takeoff position—with a substitute pilot from another crew in command of our aircraft.

The unspoken gloom hugged that aircraft with a shroud of sinister foreboding.

It turned out that Dick had taken his family on a brief tour of the island that day with full knowledge that he had plenty of time to return within the 12-hour window that we had last heard.

The catastrophe occurred when the 12-hour window changed to two hours and all crews received a phone call to assemble immediately for pre-brief.

Back in 1972, the electronic miracle called a cell phone did not exist, and until Dick returned home to a phone message left in panic by an airman, (and one from me)he had no knowledge that his crew had already departed for the base to fly the most important, and dangerous mission we had ever undertaken. Not his fault, nor anyone's. It just happened that way.

As I turned in my seat on the lower deck of the aircraft to confirm closure of the crew entry/egress hatch just before we taxied out, the most beautiful sight I could imagine appeared.

Dick had returned home, received the message and hustled to the base, and received a command staff car ride out to the aircraft, during which he was given a short-version mission brief. All of a sudden, the atmosphere inside the aircraft changed. I smiled at him and saluted. A brief glance from him and a return salute as he hustled up the ladder told me everything that could be right about that day and that mission would be.

What place fear?

It is difficult to explain, I know. But our crew became family again for this flight into a hostile world. The shroud lifted and now it became simply a life or death mission over what, at that time, was the most heavily defended city in the world. We could handle that.

Fear is not something that entered my mental process during those flights into North Vietnam. One might think it would lurk about and dominate a combat flight crewmember's thoughts about death or capture or torture. But it didn't. I honestly don't remember feeling afraid. Perhaps the training, or the necessity to just get the job done, or the organized chaos and frenetic activity level of such an endeavor pushed it aside. I don't really know. And in talking later with other crewmembers, fear had no home on that aircraft. We each had a job to do.

Coast In

"Pilot, Nav, right to 340," I called out our intended heading as we coasted in to Qui Nhon, South Vietnam after a five hour leg from Andersen including an air refueling north of the Philippines. The only sound in the aircraft was the comforting roar of the B52's eight turbojet engines. I checked my heading one more time and obtained a radar fix to update the navigation computer's position. We exited the "timing box," which allowed each three-ship formation of bombers to ensure adherence to the planned schedule. My mission as lead navigator of the formation was to get our three aircraft to the target precisely at our scheduled target time. The coordinated attack with the other 117 lumbering giants demanded precise navigation. We were on time and on course for Hanoi. My crew of six had been together for about a year. With a few practice missions at Westover A.F.B., Massachusetts, we flew a B52 non-stop from our home base to Andersen A.F.B., Guam to begin our first combat tour in November 1971. This was our third TDY tour.

Most of our B52 missions had been cakewalks—bombing the Viet Cong in the jungles of South Vietnam where the U.S. retained complete air superiority and no SAMs existed.

During successive tours, we flew out of both B52 bases in the Pacific Rim -- Andersen, and U-Tapao Air Field in Thailand. In those days, B52 crews stayed in the combat zone for four to five months, and then returned home for 28 days, followed by the next combat tour. Set up so the time in the combat zone could be called temporary duty and repeated indefinitely, it also allowed us to see our families, which kept most of us going and was a much anticipated event.

"Crew, Nav, we're twenty-five minutes south of the Gulf of Tonkin, about one hour to the target." It was also my job to advise the crew of action points since each crewmember performed critical tasks along the route of flight. Missing one of these, in hostile territory, could prove fatal. My crewmate on the windowless lower deck of the B52 was Lt. Col. Jean Beaudoin, the radar navigator and bombardier, a gray-haired Frenchman and proud of it. Together we were responsible for navigation from take-off to landing, rendezvous with the KC-135 air-to-air refueling tanker, getting to the target precisely on time, setting up the bombing system, locating the precise aiming point for our target and unloading our 54,000 pounds of weapons.

Over the Gulf of Tonkin

"Pilot, Nav, we've got a problem down here."

My navigation position counters failed. These counters showed us our position in latitude and longitude and were continually updated by the radar navigator who located a known radar return on the ground and placed a set of electronic crosshairs on it, much like an arcade video game.

"Nav, Pilot, what's your plan?"

"We have the radar. We'll go range and bearing since I can't use the counters."

This meant Jean and I would manually identify ground returns from the radarscope, plot their range and bearing from the aircraft, and initiate turns and call action points.

"How about a lead change?" was Dick's logical question. This would involve the second aircraft in our formation physically repositioning itself in front of us and taking over navigation and timing to the target. We were 10 minutes from hostile territory. Besides, it took a while to reposition these flying behemoths. My pride was a factor, too. I wanted to do this. I was trained to do it, and knew I could. I knew also that Dick could order a lead change.

"No problem. I can get us to the target." My wide-eyed side glance and shoulder shrug at Jean told him it would take both of us to accomplish this "no problem" task.

We were entering the unknown geography of hostile territory, and I knew it would be a challenge to identify radar returns, many of them built of wood, which does not reflect radar. Fortunately, our route of flight took us north over the Gulf of Tonkin where we used land/water contrast to define coastal geography. This made it easier to pick out radar returns for our range and bearing position updates.

"Rog, copy," I heard from Dick, knowing he understood what the situation was but trusted us to get the job done if we said we could. For the first time, a knot formed in my stomach.

"Crew, Nav, we're over water and into the Gulf of Tonkin." This first warning of hostile territory alerted the crew to keep a sharp eye. I heard only silence in return.

Threat Area

"Anything?" Dick asked our Electronic Warfare Officer (EW).

"Negative."

Defense of the aircraft was the EW's critical function. At his disposal was a myriad of top secret electronic jamming equipment and radar, very expensive aluminum crepe paper, and flares, both of the latter two dispensed from the aircraft to decoy incoming surface-to-air missiles (SAMs).

"Pilot, Nav, left to 290. Crew seven minutes to next turn. We're 60 miles from the coast (of North Vietnam). Seventeen minutes to target."

"EW, Nav, threat area at the turn." This informed the Electronic Warfare officer to watch for SAMs, even though I knew he was already focused on that activity.

"Crew, EW, I have launch on two, 1 o'clock and 9 o'clock. No uplink." The presence of an uplink signal meant the North Vietnamese ground radar was sending guidance signals to the missile. No uplink was one for the good guys!

"Pilot, Nav, right to 355. Crew, 20 miles from coast in. RN let's get the checklists done."

We were 70 miles from Hanoi.

"I've got a SAM!" called the pilot.

"EW has uplink."

SAMs

"OK, it's back down," said the EW, indicating that the missile lost the guidance signal.

SAMs suddenly came at us like an angry swarm of bees. We were told later that over 200 of the Russian supersonic surface-to-air missiles were fired at the seven waves of B-52s that night. Our bombers couldn't run from them. We cruised at 450 mph. The SAM cruised at 2400 mph.

That's when we heard that "Damn" from the co-pilot due to the missile that had flown between our engines on the right side. I felt for the ejection seat handle and fixated momentarily on the red ejection light that the pilot would illuminate. The navigator in the B-52 ejected first, and downward, to allow an escape hatch in case others needed to bail out manually.

"Went right between engines five and six. Couldn't have missed us by more than fifty feet. Damn."

The proximity detonation device on the SAM 2 Guideline missile caused it to explode without contact with the aircraft. If it detonated that close, our right wing would be shredded and send us spiraling to earth in a ball of flames.

I released the ejection handle and Jean and I went right back to our checklists. There was no panic in the aircraft, not in the co-pilot's voice, and not in my mind. Instantaneously, we were back at work, getting ready to unleash total destruction on the Van Dien vehicle depot, eighteen miles south of Hanoi.

The training and discipline Strategic Air Command provided for us over years of simulators and practice missions, worked. Briefly, I thought of how proud I was to be part of this professional crew. Despite SAMs, worry, tension and facing death eyeball to eyeball, no one missed a beat.

"Crew, guns" called our tail gunner, who sat in the tail of the aircraft 140 feet behind the rest of the crew.

"I have aircraft at 7o'clock, tracking." The tail gunner's armament consisted of four .50 caliber machine guns, each with 600 rounds of ammunition, and were controlled by radar which the gunner used to track and target hostile aircraft. Two North Vietnamese fighter jets were shot down by B-52 tail gunners during the eleven days.

The North Vietnamese also sent up aircraft, not to attack, but rather to track U.S. aircraft. They estimated speed, heading, and altitude of the B52's so that SAM acquisition radar could better locate and target our bombers.

"Aircraft going away," called the gunner.

"RN, Nav, not sure what that radar return is. Doesn't look like it's on the map."

Our tables downstairs looked like we pulled everything out of our nav bags and threw it up in the air. They were covered with maps, navigation plotters, checklists, stopwatches, and a variety of other navigation equipment. Amidst the mess, Jean and I methodically kept the aircraft on time and on course, completed our checklists, and prepared our minds and our stomachs for the bomb run to Hanoi.

"RN, Nav, confirm that return is Thai Binh?" The question seemed almost an aside as I plotted, studied my radar scope and computed distance and course to the next turn point

"Let's look farther out." Jean set the radar range at 100 miles and Hanoi popped up at our 11 o'clock position, right where it should be. That return was unmistakable. I stared at it for a moment wondering what it had in store for us, certain that I didn't want to know the answer.

"That's it."

"Pilot, Nav, left to 320. Crew, seven minutes to target. Radar, bomb run checklist"

The interphone chatter in the airplane was reaching climactic proportions as we neared the target area. The co-pilot, gunner, and pilot constantly called out SAM launches and clock positions. The EW confirmed SAM reports and whether or not the missiles acquired or locked on to us. Jean and I reported navigation points, times to target, and those action points for other crewmembers to perform required tasks.

It was the organized chaotic verbalization of a B52 combat

crew at war. Each flight crewmember knew exactly what needed to be done. Despite the appearance of total disorder, and the missiles constantly trying to kill us, each one successfully carried out his task.

Bomb Run

In six minutes our three-ship cell of B-52s would unload 162,000 pounds of explosives on the target, rendering it unusable to the North Vietnamese. As one crewmember said, "We had wall-to-wall SAMs every step of the way."

Our three aircraft were in an offset triangle formation, one mile and 500 feet altitude apart, as we started the bomb run. This was crucial so that the combination of defensive electronics would create a "jamming" effect on enemy radar. Instead of appearing as three separate aircraft, the North Vietnamese had to shoot at a large blob of massive energy being poured out from our combined aircraft. This tactic significantly enhanced our chances of survival.

Jean placed the electronic crosshairs on our aiming point for the target.

"Nav, confirm aim point."

I studied my radarscope for 15 seconds. "Rog, that's it."

"Pilot, RN, center the PDI." The PDI was a steering needle on the pilot's instrument panel tied into the bomb system. When centered the aircraft was aimed directly at the target.

Jean and I worked our way through the bomb run checklist to prepare the bomb system for release of the weapons. The bombs did not start the arming sequence until a wire was automatically pulled from each one as they left the racks.

"Crew, EW, multiple SAM launch 12 o'clock."

"Pilots searching."

"Bingo, have what looks like two, no three coming up from our 12 o'clock."

"Uplink!" responded the EW.

"EW, co-pilot, two tracking across."

A missile headed right for us would not change position in the pilot's windshield. "Tracking across" confirmed that two of the missiles moved across his line of sight which meant they were going somewhere else. The bad news was the third missile.

"Third one still has uplink."

"Damn, comin' straight at us," the co-pilot yelled, bone-chilling, spine-tingling words.

"Crew, starting combat turns."

The pilot put the aircraft into a series of banked turns, a tactic meant to break the missile's lock on our aircraft. The turns also diminished the effectiveness of our electronic countermeasures, but the decision, with a missile headed straight for us, was easy for the pilot to make.

"EW dispensing chaff."

In the midst of this, Jean and I finished our checklist and concentrated solely on the target which was 90 seconds away.

"I'll need straight and level at 30 seconds to go, pilot."

This was essential so that the bombing gyro stabilized prior to release of the weapons. Without the stabilization, the bombs could be tossed just about anywhere.

"Rog," was all Dick had time to say. I could hear the strain in his voice as it reflected the exhaustion of keeping this behemoth aircraft in combat turns. It was like driving a loaded cement truck with no power steering, no automatic transmission, and no brakes.

"Lost uplink," called the EW, his voice at a lower pitch. The missile missed us and wandered upward.

"Pilot, sixty seconds to target, straight and level, center the PDI," Jean calmly requested.

"Rog, straight and level, PDI centered."

"Thirty seconds to target."

"Twenty seconds to target," I counted down, rather calmly I thought.

"SAM launch dead ahead," called the EW.

"Searching," Dick said to no one in particular.

"Bingo, have it. Looks like it could hit us right between the eyes."

The missile did not move across his line of sight. We were its bull's-eye. A SAM travelling at 2400 mph would take about ten more seconds to reach the aircraft. At bombs away, that missile would impact the aircraft.

This time we couldn't execute combat turns to get out of the way. Our aircraft was a sitting duck with nowhere to hide.

"10 seconds. Bomb doors open."

We didn't open the bomb doors earlier because it created a bigger radar target for SAMs.

"EW dispensing chaff."

"Missile still tracking visually."

"Crew, prepare for bailout."

If I felt fear on this mission, those words created it.

"At bombs away, I'm gonna bend the fuselage."

The pilot was going to put the aircraft into a turn it shouldn't be able to make to avoid the missile. Again, we would expose ourselves to additional missile launches due to the degradation of our ECM, but there was no other decision to make.

"Five seconds."

"Hol---y Mother..."

"Bombs away," called the RN.

The aircraft shuddered as all the weapons departed simultaneously.

The severe turn yanked me to the right and the ejection seat shoulder straps burned into my skin through the flight suit.

Where was it? The bailout light? Where was it? Oh yeah, look up Paul. My mind was doing things my body couldn't comprehend. All in the flash of an instant. You have to go first. How can we get this far and then get blown out of the sky? Ejection D ring, find it, find it, gotta find it...there.

Keep your elbows in. Brace your back. All galloping through my mind.

Not us. Why us? Stay with me God. Tighten your seatbelt. Already did that. A voice. There's a voice. Foggy. Not making sense. A voice....

An explosion. A brilliant flash. The airplane vibrated and rocked from side to side. It detonated far enough away that there was no damage.

"Crew, Pilot, keep your eyes open. We're not out of it yet."

What did the voice mean, keep my eyes open...how could I if I was dead?

"Nav, pilot, heading?"

Heading...Heading...Nav...yeah...that's me...must not be dead...Heading...

"Crew, Radar, bomb doors closed."

What seemed like minutes of agony flashed by so quickly no one noticed my slight hesitation responding.

"Left 260."

"Everybody OK?" Dick polled the crew and got a positive response.

My god, looks like the whole world is on fire down there." Jean looked through the old, unused visual bombsight which allowed him to see below the aircraft.

"Must be what hell's like."

"Crew, Nav, 15 minutes 'til we're out of threat area."

"Stay sharp," requested the pilot.

"Oh, Christ," called the co-pilot, "visual SAM at 3 o'clock."

"SAM uplink 3 o'clock," confirmed the EW.

"Comin' at us," called the co-pilot a bit louder than before.

"EW, releasing chaff."

We never figured out why the missiles missed us, or why they didn't detonate, or why other aircraft were hit and we weren't. Those thoughts occurred to us when we learned of the crewmembers who bailed out...or worse. It didn't suppress our sense of relief however.

This one went over us and detonated a football field above our left wing. No damage.

Over the Fence

"Crew, Nav, out of the threat area."

Dick made his call to the airborne mission commander, "Over the fence with three." That told him that all three aircraft completed the mission successfully and were safely out of the threat zone. I felt the collective sense of relaxation among us.

As we turned south, the aircraft was silent. No interphone chatter, no activity, as if we entered a different dimension, peaceful and quiet. The adrenaline left my body and I sagged in my ejection seat. It was then that it all hit me, what we did, the danger, and the magnitude of it. I felt suddenly exhausted.

Later, satisfied that we weren't going to die, we coasted out of South Vietnam and headed home, six and a half hours and an air-to-air refueling away. The B52 gulped fuel with its eight engines at a rate that wouldn't give it any miles per gallon awards, even for aircraft. It did its job and needed a drink, and there was a KC-135 tanker plane out there waiting to quench its thirst.

Inside most of us broke out our flight lunches, and devoured them. And as I ate my chicken, or P&J sandwich, or whatever it was, I remember thinking that amidst all that chaos, sitting down in the "black hole" of the bottom deck, I had not seen a single missile or the night sky filled with them, or the parade of B-52s flying into North Vietnam, or the earth itself burning beneath me from the wrath let loose by our massive bombing force. In a sense I had "missed it all." Yet we were the two, the RN and Nav, that had navigated the aircraft to this spot on the globe, placed those electronic crosshairs on precisely the right radar return, connected the release circuits disconnect handle, and let loose this pandemonium and reign of death unlike most one would ever see. It seemed odd to me at the time—and does now—that it could happen that way. In a sense, I am glad it did. I don't know why. But I do know we all did our job, and did it very well, because you know what—the POWs came home a couple months later and I will always be proud of that.

Many hours later, a worn out crew landed at Andersen. The end of a fifteen hour mission. Eighteen hours including prebrief, preflight of the aircraft, the two hours it took to get seventy-eight B-52s launched from Andersen, and post-flight debrief in the base gymnasium.

Epilogue

At our debriefing we got smacked in the face with how lucky we were. Two B52's were shot down. Two good friends of Dick's and mine weren't coming back. We had played golf with them 36 hours before. That's what brought it home for me…made it personal. The thoughts of mortality and potential death came crashing down. Before, it was a mission--a dangerous one--but it was a thing, a possibility, not a dead golfing buddy you just had a pitcher of beer and a pizza with at the Officer's Club the day before.

It all welled up inside me. All I could think of was some stranger in uniform with the base chaplain by his side, walking up to their front doors back home and giving hysterical wives and crying children the devastating news. Dick and I glanced at each other for a moment and I could tell from his eyes that it crashed down on him too. We never spoke of it. We couldn't do that. There were more missions to fly. Minutes later the debrief was over and a melancholy crew left the building.

"Guys, let's hit the roach coach and get a couple chili dogs," Dick offered, "I'll buy."

So we did…and he did…and everything was back to normal, at least until we launched again for Hanoi.

Was it Worth It?

Sir Robert Thompson, noted British expert on Southeast Asian wars, thought it was. In the book The Lessons of Vietnam he is quoted as saying:

"In my view, on December 30, 1972, after eleven days of those B-52 attacks on the Hanoi area, you had won the war. It was over! They would have taken any terms. And that is why, of course, you actually got a peace agreement in January, which you had not been able to get in October."[6]

---

[6] Ibid. Linebacker II, A View from the Rock, 1985, p.173

Colonel Robinson Risner, who spent seven and one-half years in prison, said he believed the release of American POWs came about largely because of President Nixon's decision to step up bombing and the introduction of B-52 raids against the Hanoi-Haiphong area. Recalling the B-52 raids, Risner said, "On the 18th of December—I think that was the first night of the B-52 raids—there was never such joy seen in our camp before. There were people jumping up and down and putting their arms around each other, and there were tears running down our faces.

"We knew they were B-52s and that President Nixon was keeping his word and that the Communists were getting the message.

"We saw reaction in the Vietnamese that we had never seen under the attacks from fighters. They at least knew we had some weapons they had not felt and that President Nixon was willing to use those weapons in order to get us out of Vietnam."7

April, 1973

The eleven days of bombing brought the North Vietnamese back to the negotiating table. The POWs came home. Our crew was back at Andersen after going home for four weeks. No one was certain what would happen in Vietnam yet. But in the relative calm after the Christmas bombings I started an upgrade program to move over to the RN position on the B-52.

Dick and I shared the same birth month of April and took our annual flight physicals. An hour after we arrived back at our quarters, the phone rang. The doctor wanted to see Dick again.

June, 1974

Dick Purinton was dead from leukemia. I received a call at home in Ohio where I was stationed at Wright-Patterson AFB flying as an RN on the B-52H. That's what the doctor wanted to see him about. They sent him home and he died. After all we went through together, Dick was dead. I was angry with God for a very long time.

Partial Bibliography

Brig. General James R. McCarthy and Lt. Colonel George B
Allison, "Linebacker II, A View from the Rock", ed. Colonel
Robert E. Rayfield, (Maxwell Air Force Base)
<http://www.airforcehistory.hq.af.mil/Publications/fulltext/
linebacker2.pdf>

Poole, D., Operation Linebacker II. 18 December 1998.
<http://members.aol.com/dpoole1272/home/lbdays.htm>

Walter J. Boyne, "Linebacker II," Air Force Magazine Online
(November, 1997).
<http://www.afa.org/magazine/Nov1997/1197lineback.html>

Robert F. Dorr & Lindsay Peacock, Boeing's Cold War Warrior
B-52 Stratofortress, (Great Britain: Osprey Aviation, 2000).

Chris Hobson, Vietnam Air Losses, (Great Britain: Midland
Publishing, 2001

Robert M. Kipp, Counterinsurgency from 30,000 Feet, The B-52 in
Vietnam, Air University Review, January-February 1968

Last Man Out

"I don't remember anything from the time I jumped...when it was dark, until I found myself floating in the water alone, bleeding from a head wound, with my parachute stretched out behind me. I was told later I was out there in eight to ten foot shark-infested seas for four-and-a-half hours. It wasn't until ten years later that I learned how close I came to not being rescued."
~Lt. Col. Myles McTernan, USAF (retired)

"I thought to myself before I ejected, "After I pull this trigger, I will either be alive or dead. In total darkness, I couldn't determine whether or not I was blind. I had blood in my eyes. Then the first thing I saw was the B-52 exploding when it hit the water. For a few moments I thought we were over land and could be POWs."
~ Capt. William Milcarek, Co-pilot, Ruby Two

Since the maiden flight of the first B-52A production model on August 8, 1954, only eighteen have fallen to enemy fire. This is the account of the last B-52 shot down in the Vietnam war and the story of Lt. Colonel Gerald Wickline's crew, and its navigator, Captain Myles McTernan—the Last Man Out.

∞

This was not Lt. Col Jerry Wickline's crew's first sortie into hostile night skies filled with deadly surface-to-air missiles fired by the North Vietnamese. They had adopted the tactic of launching the

SAM's as a "wall" because it was the only way the enemy could shoot down any of our B-52s. The reason was because a three-ship cell of the aircraft on a bombing mission could envelop all three ships in a giant blob of defensive radar energy which was fairly successful in masking each individual airplane.

Wickline's crew had been home for their 28 day break from the war when the Christmas bombings began on December 18th, 1972. They deployed back to Guam on Christmas Day and flew their first flight into Hanoi on December 27th. Though they missed the massed bombing campaign of the 26th that we discussed in our previous story, *Over the Fence*, all hell broke loose on the 27th as the enemy spent its frustration on the B-52s that decimated their capital city the night before.

But it's better if Jerry Wickline tells the story from his picture window view at the front of a B-52 being showered from below with SAMs.

"You can't believe how bad it was," says Wickline. "Our target was a railroad yard on the north side of Hanoi. We came in from over the water just north of Haiphong, and we no more than coasted in over land when the first missiles were fired and they continued in barrages for the next 23 minutes until we exited the SAM rings near the Laos border.

"We saw well over 100 SAM's fired and more than 30 of them came within one mile of our airplane, with at least half of those missing us by less than 200 feet.

"My mouth was so full of cotton I could barely talk, and the whole time, I thought I would be dead the next second. There was no way to outmaneuver them, and several times I was blinded by a near missile detonation or from the brilliant glare of their rocket trail as they went past me.

"The B-52 right behind me was shot down, with no survivors listed as of this time. The total time of the mission was 16 ½ hours with one pre-strike and one post-strike refueling."

The crew's second mission over Hanoi, flown after only 16 hours of crew rest, on Dec. 29th was no picnic either. Wickline again describes it:

"This time we were hitting Phuc Yen airfield (NW of Hanoi) and flew practically the same route. This mission was a milk run compared to the one before. Only about 40 missiles were fired and only about eight came within one mile of us, and none very close.

"We did have a Mig close to within 3 miles at our 12 o'clock, but he never locked on or fired any missiles. We thought he had the first plane in our cell, because he was only about a mile from him when he broke off the attack.

"On this raid, we had three waves of B-52s striking the same target, from three different axes at the same target time. We were more afraid of another B-52 dropping bombs on us than we were of SAM's and Migs because we were at 31,000 feet and the lowest altitude of the three waves. Anyhow, no one was shot down or even hit that night, and that was the last raid over Hanoi.

"This mission was only 14 hours long and as soon as we landed, we were shoved on a KC-135 to go to U-Tapao. So we had Christmas in Guam and New Years in Thailand."

Wickline's crew was exhausted, relieved, and happy to be alive after thirty combat hours in the air, plus a long trip from Andersen AFB, Guam to their new station at U-Tapao Airfield, Thailand.

From there they were scheduled to continue to fly missions into North and South Vietnam. The first one, the night of 3 Jan 1973, was considered a "milk run" by Wickline's crew after their two missions over Hanoi where they had faced so many SAMs that Wickline said they looked like "swarms of fireflies."

This mission was to bomb a truck park 15 miles northwest of Vinh, a North Vietnamese coastal city which was located on the main north-south highway and rail line midway between Hanoi and Hue, the northernmost city of South Vietnam.

The whole crew figured it had to be easier and safer than the bombing raids of Linebacker II where more than one thousand SAMs fired shot down fifteen B52s. They would learn later that thirty-two of those crewmembers were killed-in-action, and thirty-five became prisoner's-of-war.

Their aircraft, call sign Ruby Two, was part of a nine-ship wave of B-52s

"We saw lots of triple A fire over Vinh," Wickline recalled, "more than I ever saw before, including the two missions over Hanoi. Several missiles were fired at planes ahead of us, and at the other two waves of B52s hitting targets west and southwest of Vinh."

"We were next to last in the string of aircraft," said Myles McTernan, Wickline's navigator and now an experienced combat crewmember of Ruby Two.

"I wasn't happy to be next to last. We'd learned from previous missions that the SAM operators aligned their sights on the first few aircraft. By the time the last planes flew over, they were able to aim their missiles more accurately. But I told myself not to worry; it was a milk run, and we were veterans of Linebacker II."

Wickline adds, "At about the IP (Initial Point is where the crew begins the bomb run) we picked up some SAM signals and started our SAM maneuvers. Several missiles were fired at planes ahead of us, and at the other two waves of B-52's which were hitting targets West and SW of Vinh."

"At forty seconds to go before bombs away, the co-pilot and I saw the distant flashes of four SAMs off their left wing. All the missiles appeared stationary in the windshield, which meant the SAMs were tracking directly at us.

"SAM's #1 and #2 were fired first followed a few seconds later by #3and #4. I maneuvered to avoid #1 and #2 with #1 going past our nose (real close) and detonating just above us (going up). . Technical Sergeant Carlos S. Killgore, our tail gunner, reported the second missile missed our tail by only fifty feet, and exploded just above us.

"I had lost sight of #3 and #4, but it didn't matter. There was no time left to dodge. We were ten seconds from the target, and I needed to fly straight and level to get an accurate bomb drop, so I rolled level with the PDI centered and, simultaneously with bombs away, we were rocked by a tremendous explosion directly below our nose.

"Ruby Two was the bull's-eye," Wickline said.

As the last of one hundred and eight five-hundred-pound bombs fell from the aircraft, one of the unseen missiles had found its target.

"Three windows on my side of the airplane shattered and showered us with broken bits of glass. The #1 engine fire light came on and a blazing fire was burning in the #1 pod. We shut #1 down. All of my flight instruments, including airspeed and attitude were inoperative. Most of the engine instruments on both sides of the cockpit were inoperative; in fact the glass was shattered in most of them. All hydraulic power to the left wing was out and all fuel gauges on the left wing were either spinning or stuck."

Co-pilot Bill Milcarek tried to relate what the experience of being hit by a SAM was like. "Imagine you are in a giant light bulb which has been thrown to the floor. It was a very loud "pop" sound, then almost a ringing in your ears which made things quiet for a few seconds. Everyone seemed calm after the impact. I was too concerned about procedures to have time to be scared."

Wickline added, "I polled the crew. Everyone answered except Sergeant Killgore."

On the lower deck, fifteen feet behind and eight feet below Wickline, catastrophe struck quickly. A fuel transfer valve above the head of Major Roger A. Klingbeil, the radar-navigator, was destroyed by shrapnel and highly flammable JP-4 fuel poured out, soaking Klingbeil and McTernan, leaving severe chemical burns on their exposed skin. Major Klingbeil, the most severely burned, screamed in pain.

"The Nav and RN reported that the lower deck was floating in jet fuel," said Wickline. "I worried if they could get out. The escape hatches were filled with JP-4. Any tiny spark could ignite the fumes and destroy the aircraft."

"We didn't even want to shut down our equipment on the lower deck," said McTernan, "because we were afraid moving a switch could create that spark."

"Three more SAM's passed across our nose and exploded just

above us," Wickline reported. "We got out over water and turned south."

Wickline remembers that the airplane was barely controllable.

"Every time I attempted to slow down, it would start a roll to the right and could only be straightened out by gaining airspeed.

"The fire in the number one pod continued to burn intermittently, and I lost control over the number eight engine throttle. I think it was running at idle. As near as I could tell, the other six engines were working okay, but I didn't have reliable instruments, so I couldn't be sure."

Soon after the explosion, Wickline handed the aircraft to Milcarek. His entire windshield was cracked and shattered and they had to have a visual on Ruby One because they had no flight instruments. They only changed the radio frequency for fear of causing an explosion from the fuel fumes emanating from the flooded lower deck.

"Only two or three engine throttles remained connected to the engines," said Milcarek. "All others were severed. I was still flying the aircraft when we leveled the aircraft at 12,000 feet bailout altitude. While the A/C read the bail-out checklist, I noticed the aircraft controls feeling mushy which indicated we were nearing a stall so I pushed up all the throttles, locked them, and forgot about them.

"We probably bailed out at excessive airspeed which (may) have caused (some) of the injuries" added Milcarek. "All of us had neck strains, and huge bruises between our thighs from the sudden and violent opening of our chutes due to zero-delay lanyards being attached since we thought that the aircraft could explode upon anyone's ejection."

Wickline continued. "We tried continuously to contact the gunner, but to no avail. We started a descent with the other two airplanes staying with us, and leveled off at 12,000 feet about 90 miles north of Da Nang. Soon after level off, we felt a thump and heard a parachute beeper go off.

Our gunner had bailed out all on his own, as flames from a fire in the belly began licking around his turret. That was one of the smartest things the gunner ever did, as had I not heard from him I may have tried to land the airplane and would surely have killed us all. Once I was sure the rescue forces were in contact with the gunner, we started setting up for the bailout.

Wickline and Milcarek struggled to keep the plane in the air for the next half hour as they flew south toward the safety of the seventeenth parallel, which marked the demarcation between the two warring Vietnams.

"As soon as I heard over the radio that rescue forces from the U.S.S. Saratoga were in contact with Sergeant Killgore, I turned out to sea and ordered bailout about 20 miles east of Da Nang."

On the lower deck the spilled fuel still worried McTernan.

"I tried not to think that the entire airplane could become an instant fireball if the ejection seat rockets ignited the fumes filling the cockpit. I pulled my parachute straps so tight, I must have looked like Popeye."

With no more room for safety, Colonel Wickline fired up the big red warning light and called, "Bailout, Bailout, Bailout" over the interphone.

Despite his concerns over the spilled fuel, McTernan yanked the trigger ring between his legs and shot back and downward. Klingbeil ejected at the same time.

Upstairs, Wickline reports, "I heard two thumps which I assumed was the navigator and RN ejection seats firing, followed a few seconds later by a third, which was the EW. I told the co-pilot to go and he squeezed the trigger. I was temporarily blinded by flying debris. After I got my eyes cleared and looked, he was gone.

"Thank God, there was no fireball," said Wickline.

McTernan's hatch hadn't blown as it was supposed to, and, instead of exiting the plane, he came to a dead halt.

"I heard the ejection seat rocket and felt the seat accelerate briefly, but there was no wind blast or ruffle of the parachute, and I felt no separation. I opened my eyes and saw the hatch must have been jammed by shrapnel from the missile explosion."

Wickline made a last call on interphone to confirm none of the crew members were on board. "When no one responded, I waited a few interminable seconds, pulled the throttles to idle, and ejected."

What Wickline didn't know was that a desperate Captain McTernan could not reach his microphone switch.

"I heard Wickline call, 'Anyone still onboard?' I realized he didn't know I was downstairs, but I couldn't key my mike in time to tell him. As I reached for the foot switch, I heard the co-pilot eject, and I panicked. I wrestled with the seatbelt so I could let Wickline know my predicament. I took a few seconds to get loose and climbed up to the platform between the downstairs seats. That's when I heard Wickline eject, and my heart jumped into my throat."

Wickline said he felt a tremendous kick in the seat of his pants, a great blast of cold air, severe tumbling, and an extremely sharp jolt, which tore the ejection seat from his hands, then a loud pop, followed by a very intense silence.

"It all happened in seconds. I looked up, saw that beautiful big orange and white canopy above my head, and said, 'Wickline, you lucky son of a gun. You've got it made now.' Then I pulled off my oxygen mask and barfed into the South China Sea a few thousand feet below. I think it came from the relief of the last 30 minutes, and that I was away from that airplane, which was a fireball waiting to happen.

"It took about 15 minutes or so to come down from 12,000 feet in the parachute and it was so quiet that it almost made your ears hurt. I saw a fireball on the horizon. Our B-52 had hit the water and exploded. I started to oscillate in the parachute, swinging from side to side, so I reached up to grab the risers to stop the oscillations and could barely get my right arm above my head, and when I did, it hurt like hell. I had to do this three or four times during the descent, and each time my right shoulder hurt worse and by the time I hit the water, my right arm was useless and very painful. I started hearing the sound of waves, and as I had already deployed my survival kit, I uncovered my parachute quick disconnect covers and got ready to hit the water. As my feet hit I released my parachute and barely bobbed below the surface."

McTernan remained alone in the aircraft. The huge Stratofortress was on fire and, with the throttles set to idle began a slow arcing plunge toward the sea now only ten thousand feet below. There were only seconds to get out, or he would die when it hit the water if not sooner.

But he didn't yet have a parachute he could wear to escape the plunging, burning inferno. He frantically searched for the spare chute that was aboard for extra crewmembers…and found it. But he didn't know what altitude he was at or how many seconds until the plane crashed into the sea.

"My only hope was to bail out through the hole left by the radar navigator's ejection seat escape hatch. I crouched above it, rolled into a ball, and fell through the hole into total darkness. I knew I bailed out a couple minutes behind the rest of the crew, and I'd land in the water miles from them. Though I remember nothing, I must have pulled the rip cord.

"I didn't have a life raft; it was part of the ejection seat survival kit back on the aircraft. Only my life vest kept me from drowning in ten foot swells while I waited for rescue. My last hope was that the choppers would come quickly."

As he floated down, Wickline had remembered he left his favorite cigarette lighter in the tray by his window. "I got furious at my forgetfulness, but that passed quickly as I glanced at the horizon and saw Ruby Two explode in a huge reddish orange fireball."

Somewhere on the pitching sea between Wickline and the fireball, McTernan lost all track of time.

"When I woke up it was daylight. My chute floated behind me, my life preserver had inflated, and I was covered with blood. I couldn't remember anything and thought I must have lost consciousness, but later they diagnosed it as pain amnesia."

Wickline was having his own less serious difficulties.

"It took me about fifteen agonizing minutes to claw my way into the life raft as waves as high as a house washed over me. Then I discovered I crawled into the narrow end, which made the raft very unstable. I held on as I got tossed about, pulled out my survival radio, turned it on, and waited.

"I heard nothing for a while, and then I heard my co-pilot talking to an OV-10 pilot so I knew they were looking for us. About this time the sun came up, and with it the wind, which made the waves higher and chilled me to the bone. There was a low overcast and lots of haze, with very poor visibility. The co-pilot continued to talk to the OV-10, giving him short counts for ADF and soon after, I heard an engine, and looked up to see an OV-10 approaching. He passed over me first, so I gave him a call and he set up an orbit directly over me, and started to direct the helicopter, which was already airborne, to the area.

"About an hour after I hit the water, I saw the helicopter, and watched while he picked up the co-pilot who was only about 200 yards from me. Then he came over and picked me up. Even though my arm hurt like hell, I attached myself to the rescue devise with a deathlike grip and was hoisted into the helicopter.

"We were flown directly to the Da Nang hospital. About an hour passed before Wickline, Milcarek, Klingbeil, and Fergason were rescued by helicopter and flown to Da Nang Air Base hospital where they met up with Killgore.

"My co-pilot was in good shape," Wickline said. The USS Saratoga rescued the gunner and he reported no injuries. Roger Klingbeil suffered from blistering JP-4 burns. Bill Fergason had a piece of helmet visor in his right eye, which must have shattered during ejection, but with no permanent damage."

Still no word on McTernan who drifted many miles away in a life or death struggle with the elements.

"For four and a half hours I attempted to use the survival equipment. Nothing worked, and I wasn't doing much to help myself, either. I lost two radios and couldn't ignite the two flare/smoke canisters. Somehow, I punctured my life preserver and needed to constantly re-inflate it by mouth."

With no way to let rescuers know where he was, barely afloat in the raging sea, McTernan said he knew death "might be only minutes away."

The right side of his face, injured during bailout, was smashed in. He was bleeding, burned by jet fuel, and had cuts on all of his fingers. His insides were a mess from all the salt water he ingested, and McTernan, told later the waters around him were shark-infested, could only wonder how he survived.

According to Milcarek, Myles, or "Mush" as the crew called him, was AWOL (absent without leave) for about five hours.

"We were all solemn due to concern for him. It was a great relief when he finally showed up in Da Nang in the hospital. I noticed that he had a large cut across his left cheek and his eye was bandaged over. He was rather blue in color from exposure floating around at sea in only a May West (life vest) without a radio in 15-foot shark infested seas.

"I said to him, 'Myles, you look like s***! He said 'Yea, I had a rough day (pause). Do I get a Purple Heart for this?' I said that I thought so. He retorted, isn't that worth three points on the civil service exam? Typical smart-ass Myles.'"

"Believe it or not," McTernan said recently while managing a slight smile, "my parents even got a telegram saying I was missing in action."

Not until ten years later at Mather Air Force Base near Sacramento, California, did McTernan learn how very close he came to going from Missing in Action to Killed in Action.

"A fellow officer and I were sharing war stories. We discovered that he worked in command support at Da Nang at the time of my rescue. He told me the small fixed-wing aircraft searching for me turned back when its fuel approached the level he needed to make it home. As the craft made the turn to return to base, the pilot saw a spot of color on the ocean. I must have just hit the top of a wave and became briefly visible. The pilot radioed a helicopter to pick me up."

McTernan looked thoughtful and added, "If that rescue plane ran out of fuel a few seconds later or earlier, or if the pilot made a right turn instead of left, or if I wasn't at the top of the wave at the right instant, I never would have been found."

*

Capt. Myles McTernan, now Lt. Col. (retired), fully recovered from his injuries. He went back to Southeast Asia in 1973 and 1974 flying training missions. In 1975 he completed his B52 tour at Dyess AFB, Texas. He then served as an instructor and flight commander in Navigator-Bombardier Training (NBT), at Mather AFB, Sacramento, California.

He was assigned, in 1980, to the FB-111 aircraft as a Radar Navigator at Pease AFB, New Hampshire. He completed his tour there as Chief of Plans in the Bomb Nav branch.

1986 found him headed back to Mather as Assistant Operations Officer for the 450th[h] training squadron, Joint Navigator Training. His appointment as Chief of Navigation Training for Joint Navigator Training at Mather closed out his career.

*

During his earlier career, Lt. Col Wickline, beginning in 1954, flew as a navigator on the RC-121 aircraft at McClellan AFB, Sacramento, California. He went back through flight school and earned his pilot's wings in 1959, then on to B52s at Travis AFB, CA. In the late 1960's he transferred to B-58s at Bunker Hill AFB, Indiana.

Wickline flew 0-2s as an Air Liaison Officer in Vietnam during 1969-1970 and then returned to B-52s at Dyess AFB, Texas until his retirement in 1973.

He and his wife live in Palm City, Florida, own a forty-foot trawler and make several pleasure voyages each year to the Bahamas. "It's a tough life," says Wickline.

*

Bill Milcarek became the youngest Aircraft Commander in the Strategic Air Command (SAC). Following his recovery from DNIF (duty not involving flying) status, SAC decided that they were behind in upgrading a co-pilot to Aircraft Commander.

"Since I was the only D-model co-pilot in SAC at the time," explains Milcarek, "I was selected to enter the upgrade program. At the time I had a total of about 800 hours flying time."

Bill has lived and worked in Manhattan since 1974. He has four grown children and three grandsons, and remains heavily involved in Veterans affairs.

∞

My thanks to Myles McTernan, Bill Milcarek, and Gerald Wickline for their co-operation and for allowing me to use their first-hand accounts of this flight. Without their courage under fire, steadfast determination to survive a deadly encounter, and willingness to recount it many years after, this story may have never been read. That would have been a shame.

∞

The B52 aircraft was designed and built to be a war machine. It has been this country's mainstream long-range strategic bomber since the mid-1950's and has been so successful that many experts predict it will continue into the 2040s, at least.

The B52D model, the aircraft Lt. Col. Wickline's crew was flying when it went down was the workhorse bomber of the Vietnam War. The B52G and B52H models flew in Desert Storm, Afghanistan, and the war in Iraq.

Some statistics:

170 B52Ds were produced

First D model flown on 4 June 1956

Six crewmembers

Eight Pratt & Whitney J57-P-19W turbojet engines

Length 156'7"

Wingspan 185' (longer than Wright Bros. first flight)

Maximum take-off weight 450,000 pounds

Empty weight 172,000 lbs.

Internal fuel 41,550 gal. (approx. 260,000 lbs)

External fuel 3,000 gal. (approx. 18,000 lbs)

Service ceiling 55,000 feet

Armament 4 x .50 caliber guns

Offensive payload 54,000 pounds

Max speed 551 knots (650 mph); Normal cruise speed approx.
450 knots
Combat radius 3012 nautical miles w/no air-to-air refueling

Bibliography

Chris Hobson, Vietnam Air Losses, (England: Midland,
      2001),   pp. 247,268.
Helicopter Losses During the Vietnam War.
      <http://www.vhpa.org/heliloss.pdf>
Robert Dorr & Lindsay Peacock, B-52 Stratofortress, (Great
      Britain: Osprey, 2000), pp.230, 235.
Gerald F. Wickline, Personal letter, written at Palm City, FL.
Myles McTernan, "Last One," The Navigator
      (April, 1987), p.12.
Myles McTernan & Gerald Wickline, Personal Interviews,
      Nov. 2003 - Feb. 2004.
Myles McTernan, "Ruby 2, 3 Jan 73," Tape recording of radio
      calls between Ruby 2 and other aircraft.
Bill Milcarek, Personal notes written exclusively for this story
      (August, 2013)

The B-52H is the only model still flying. The B-52 D model
that Wickline, Milcarek, and McTernan flew was retired in 1983.

Capt. Myles McTernan – U-Tapao Flight Line, 1972

Lt. Col. Myles McTernan

**The Last Man Out
Retirement
2008**

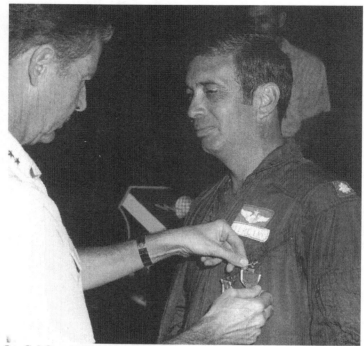

Lt. Col Gerald Wickline – Aircraft Commander Ruby Two awarded the Purple Heart in 1973

OV-10 aircraft similar to the one that spotted most of the crew of Ruby Two in the South China Sea.

Bill Milcarek – Co-pilot
Andersen AFB, Guam   January 1973

Bill Milcarek - 2010

The USS Saratoga sent out a helicopter to rescue TSGT Carlos S. Killgore, the gunner from Ruby Two. It returned hours later to pick up Capt. McTernan.

A Cessna L-19/O-1 Bird Dog aircraft similar to this one spotted Capt. McTernan bobbing on top of a wave as it turned toward home to refuel.

For the following story **Non-stop Around the World**...a
Special Dedication:

To Angelyn, who kept the pride and to her Dad, Wayne, and two B-52 crews who earned it flying a unique and hazardous mission into hostile skies at a dangerous time in a politically violent world.

Non-Stop Around the World
Crossing Gaddafi's Line of Death

"Of course we were curious when we heard we were under consideration for the Mackay, so we started checking around. I don't remember the particulars, but apparently our competition that year was a daring helicopter rescue at sea... In a way, I was almost cheering for the helicopter crew. They had done something truly heroic. We had done something demanding and impressive, and I thought we did it with great precision and professionalism, but our feat was not all that life-threatening."

~Former Capt. Wayne Hesser, Lead RN, Non-stop Around the World B-52 Flight

A rendezvous with the Soviet Navy, clearances not received for over flight of some nations, lack of VHF communications, five in-flight refuelings each from multiple tanker aircraft, 43 hours of fatigue, and hoping not to get shot down over Libya or Egypt. Sounds like a piece of cake for professional air crews of the Strategic Air Command.

Not all that life-threatening? Perhaps not in the crew's perspective but the political and diplomatic situation around the globe in 1980 was anything but settled.

That year belonged to an era long before the Berlin Wall came down, the Soviet Empire collapsed, and joint Russian-American space flights became commonplace.

The U.S. suffered a miserable economic situation with 16% inflation and interest rates through the ceiling, and the only hope in sight was a western actor named Ronald Reagan who was elected President as the decade turned from the hippie-driven 70's to the unknowns of the 80's.

But it was not only a dismal economic situation in the U.S. More significantly it was that perilous era steeped in the Cold War and just waiting for the next international incident.

The World was a Dangerous Place
LIBYA

In 1973 Libyan leader Muammar Gadaffi claimed that the entire Gulf of Sidra in the Mediterranean Sea belonged to Libya at 32 degrees, 30 minutes North Latitude with an exclusive 62 nautical mile fishing zone. He dubbed this "The Line of Death." The United States Navy deployed aircraft carrier groups in the Gulf of Sidra claiming that only the standard 12-nautical mile territorial limit applied from Libya's shoreline.

By 1979, the U.S. placed Libya on its list of state sponsors of terrorism. At the end of that year a demonstration torched the U.S. Embassy in Tripoli.

In 1980, Libyan fighters began intercepting U.S. fighter jets over the Mediterranean.

In 1981, President Reagan declared Gaddafi an "international pariah" and the "mad dog of the Middle East."

IRAN

November, 1979. Sixty-six Americans working in the U.S. Embassy in Teheran were taken hostage. The U.S. cut diplomatic ties with Iran and imposed sanctions in April, 1980. Shortly after that, eight U.S. servicemen were killed when a helicopter and a transport plane collided during a failed attempt to rescue the hostages.

IRAQ

In 1980 Iraq's Saddam Hussein invaded Iran over border disputes. The war lasted for eight years, killed 450,000, and accomplished nothing.

ITALY

Aerolinee Itavia Flight 870, a commercial McDonnell Douglas DC-9, departed Bologna for Palermo, Sicily on 27 June 1980 with 77 passengers, two pilots and two flight attendants. The aircraft crashed into the Tyrrhenian Sea, 70 nautical miles southwest of Naples, Italy 50 minutes later.

Suspicions at the time were that it was brought down by a missile. This was not confirmed until 2013 after several investigations indicated it may have been a stray Italian or French air force missile attempting to fire on a Libyan fighter, or an Israeli Mossad downing.

EGYPT

In 1981 Anwar Sadat was assassinated by Muslim extremists.

SOVIET UNION

In 1980 the Soviet Union invaded Afghanistan, and Polish workers led by Lech Walesa staged an uprising at the Gdansk shipyards. The workers won a major victory. It was the first step in the eventual dissolution of the Soviet Union.

Ronald Reagan was elected President of the U.S. and almost immediately declared the Soviet Union an "evil empire."

Robert Kaiser of ForeignAffairs.com said of that era, *"Soviet-American relations can now be divided neatly into two historical periods, both of them ended. The first lasted for a quarter-century after WWII, and was typified by what the Soviets called—disdainfully but also enviously—American diplomacy for a "position of strength." During those years the United States was unmistakably the stronger power, but somehow its superior strength did not create a satisfactory Soviet-American relationship. Then in 1972 the policies of both nations changed. The United States granted the Soviets the symbolic status of equal superpower, and that was the beginning of the second period, labeled 'détente.' In 1980 both countries decided that it, too, was unsatisfactory, so they terminated it. The significance of 1980 is indisputable."*

1979 to 1983 became the scariest era in over two decades, culminating in the shoot down by Soviet fighter jets of Korean Air Lines Flight 007 in August, 1983. The world edged closer to the brink during this era than it had when the Cuban missile crisis of the '60s almost brought the world to Armageddon.

Sending a Message

If one would believe that this 1980 around-the-world B-52 flight occurred randomly at this time to "buzz" the Soviet Navy, edge over Gadaffi's Line of Death, and perform a low-level flyover of the USS Nimitz aircraft carrier, even our brief study of the world situation at the time would tend to change a mind here and there. There was purpose, intent, and a clear message sent along with those two B-52 crews.

Fourteen courageous flight crewmembers—two typical SAC crews launched off alert status with minimal preparation as they would in a crisis—undertook to fly nonstop around the world in two B-52 aircraft and once again display that the United States global military capability to strike targets anywhere on the globe at any time remained undiminished.

It was an important statement at a crucial time in world events, and SAC HQ began planning the mission months before the crews were selected. It was then proclaimed loudly as the two strategic bombers thundered down the runway at KI Sawyer AFB, Michigan and into what could become at any time, hostile skies.

This is the story of that time, that tense Cold War era, and one glorious flight...

A Little History-The First Time Around the World

In January, 1957, when the B-52, the U.S. frontline strategic bomber, was in its infancy, five B models took off from Castle AFB near Merced, California. Three aircrews completed a non-stop flight around the globe to prove to the world that the United States Air Force's global reach and ability to strike targets was indeed worldwide. Operation Power Flite was the designated name for that mission.

The 45 hour and 19 minute, 24,235 nautical mile flight went off without a hitch until their landing sight, Castle AFB, was socked in by fog and they had to divert to March AFB in southern California.

General Curtis LeMay, then commander of Strategic Air Command (SAC) decorated each flight crewmember with the Distinguished Flying Cross (DFC) as they departed the aircraft after the flight. They had shattered the previous around-the-world nonstop mission set by a B-50 in 1949 by more than half. That record would stand until 1980.

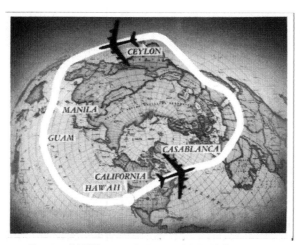

Route of 1957 around-the-world B-52 flight

The three B-52Bs that completed Operation Power Flite in 1957 prepare to depart March AFB for their home base at Castle AFB, California

Today...A Piece of Cake...Not So Much in 1980

With today's aircraft avionics capabilities and computer technology, flights around the world are commonplace. Pinpoint inertial systems and GPS allow a modern airplane to find itself anywhere in the world within a few hundred feet. Coordination of flight planning is a snap with computer-generated flight plans and charts, and country over flight clearances automatically distributed in each country. Worldwide satellite communications make coordination simple.

But at the time of this flight, even with the help of SAC planning, for a B-52 crew to overcome these obstacles, locate and perform surveillance on Soviet naval ships half a world away, rendezvous with multiple air tankers, locate a single U.S. carrier in the Indian Ocean and continue home around the other half of the globe while tired and mentally drained, was a feat of super airmanship by all aboard.

As indicated previously, this story is told mostly from the perspective of the only crewmember we could locate—Major Wayne Hesser, (USAF, ret.) Radar Navigator of the lead B-52. We were fortunate in that because the former Captain Hesser proved to be a workaholic in obtaining information about the flight, facts that we would have no other access to, and relationships among the crew. Since Hesser was responsible for navigation around the world, rendezvous with the in-flight refueling aircraft, and locating and surveying the Russian ships as well as the USS Nimitz, he proved to be the right source and was more than up to the task, and we thank him for that.

We also used some quotes from a Combat Crew Magazine article (June, 1980) written by the crew under the name of their Aircraft Commander (AC), Maj. William Thurston. We were not able to locate Maj. Thurston for this story but did pull some of his quotes from that article.

Planning Phase – 1980

Hesser describes what happened when his crew, one of two senior flight crews in the B-52 wing at KI Sawyer AFB, first learned they were being considered for the yet unknown mission.

"We were on normal nuclear alert when we were pulled off to meet with the wing commander," Hesser said."It was all rather mysterious and we were naturally a bit curious. When we met with him we were told that they wanted crews for a "special mission" and wanted to know if we were up to a very long flight.

"Well, who says no to such as offer? Sure we were up to a long flight, especially if it might offer some diversion from the grinding cycle of alert duty and training flights.

"Since we were finishing an alert tour, we were given a chance to go home and pack to fly to Omaha the next day. I don't remember exactly what I told Lin (his wife) about why we were taken off alert and where we were going, but she'd been an Air Force wife long enough to know better than to ask."

"So they bundled us off to SAC Headquarters at Offutt on a commercial flight. By this point it was starting to sink in that this was going to be something special. The trip to Omaha was exciting for us since most of us had never before seen SAC HQ or the legendary SAC underground complex.

"I don't recall exactly who hosted us, but it was the headquarters version of what we would call "Current Ops." at the base level. I remember we were shown into a briefing room where there was an easel with something covered by a curtain. After giving us an appropriate welcome someone threw back the curtain. I could tell by their smiles that they were expecting a reaction from us, and I don't think we disappointed them. I know my jaw was on the floor as I looked at a route map showing a line that went completely around the world."

The map shown them depicted a nonstop flight that started from their home base of KI Sawyer AFB, Michigan, overflew the North Atlantic, Europe , the Mediterranean Sea, across Northeast Africa, the Arabian Peninsula and into the Indian Ocean to survey ships of the Soviet Navy and rendezvous with the US carrier Nimitz.

And that was only the first half of the mission. They would then proceed to fly south of India into their fourth air-to-air refueling, over the Philippines and then northeast towards Japan, the North Pacific, across the breadth of Canada and the U.S. and home to KI Sawyer. It was breathtaking to say the least...over 43 hours around the world.

That first afternoon at SAC, the crew, along with the SAC planners, discussed potential problems with a 40+ hour flight. They took a long, detailed look at each segment of the mission.

"The SAC staff had already laid out the mission and planned it pretty thoroughly. They had anticipated more than we had the wits to figure out. We were impressed. We spent a couple days with them at Offutt planning the mission.

"Some of the route was plotted on the standard high-level 1-to-2-million JNC charts. The new version, which included precision radar fix points, had just come out. In addition to what was pre-printed, they had added several other fix points close to our route to give us additional updates for the SRAM INS we would use for navigation. Other portions of the mission were plotted on the even smaller-scale GNC charts

"SAC took our inputs and put together computer flight plans for the whole mission. Today every Sunday pilot with a Cessna has one, but back in 1980 such things were still somewhat exotic, and we were, once again, quite impressed.

"Our AC, Major Bill Thurston was named Mission Commander because he was the senior of the two AC's. Both he and the other AC, Maj. John Durham wanted the position of lead aircraft and Mission Commander, so Bill generously offered to toss a coin...and won. That's how we got the lead."

Navigation

So that all readers understand what Hesser is talking about when he describes the SRAM INS (Inertial Navigation System), and the use and importance of it on this mission, he offered the following explanation:

"The SRAM was the Short Range Attack Missile, the nuclear-tipped missile B52s carried on a rotary launcher in the aft bomb bay. Obviously, we carried no missiles on our flight, but we did have the SRAM's INS, which was fairly accurate by 1980 standards. It was usable whether missiles were loaded or not. Before we had the SRAM inertial system, our only automated navigation was a very unreliable, largely analog, dead-reckoning system...

" The B-52's bombing-navigation system was primitive by today's standards, supported by the "pots and cans," i.e., racks of amplifiers the size of beer cans with cables with canon plugs tying them into the system. Part of this system was that electronic dead-reckoning capability which we referred to as "the counters" because the position coordinates were displayed by latitude and longitude numbers on mechanical wheels which the navigator would manually plot on his chart. The radar was also the old analog system where a sweep on a CRT would paint images that then started fading away until they were refreshed by the next sweep. It was a far cry from the smart, digital, phased-array radars of today that can see several times as much with a fraction of the power.

"The B-52's large ten-inch radar display had movable crosshairs that the RN could position with a joystick called a "tracking handle." These crosshairs were used both for position updates and for bombing. To update our position, we would dial the coordinates of a fix point into the computer and position the radar crosshairs on that point. The system would then triangulate on the fix point to determine the position of the aircraft. Similarly, for bombing a non-radar-reflective target, we could feed the computer the coordinates of the target and the coordinates of a nearby aim point that was a good radar reflector. We would the put the crosshairs on the aim point, and the computer would figure out the position of the aircraft relative to the target, account for heading and wind, and send steering signals to guide us to the target and tell us when to release the bomb.

"A problem with this kind of offset bombing was that it required a precise heading. Aiming points were sometimes many miles from the target, and even a small heading error could greatly impact the accuracy. To improve the reliability of the system, the H-model bomb-nav system had the AJN-8 heading and stabilization system. This was a complicated piece of machinery with gyros and accelerometers in all three axis that provided very stable heading and attitude information when it worked. The problem was that it was a bit sensitive and often dumped, especially when you were trying to do the initial alignment on the ground (which it required). About the only equipment failure we experienced on our mission was the loss of our AJN-8 when we had a bit of bad communication and our pilot taxied before our system was aligned. It crashed as soon as the airplane started to move, and there was no resurrecting it.

" So we flew around the world using our backup heading system: the "coffee can." This was a single gyro, but a large one, in a unit about the size of a coffee can (hence the name), which was actually the primary system on older airplanes, so it was fairly adequate, especially when we were able to periodically adjust it with heading updates from the SRAM inertial system.

" This older heading system was typical of the engineering in the old Buff. In the days before technology and digital magic could overcome any obstacle, brute force was often substituted. Gyros tend to drift. Build a big one that would have more of Newton's laws working in its favor. Radar systems had many inherent errors because of the size of the transmitted beam? Build a bigger antenna so the beam would be more focused.

"Of course we also had the sextants which we elected not to use to make the point that with accurate inertial systems coming in it was time to start thinking of these venerable old navigation instruments as museum pieces. Of course we took out our sextants and checked them, but that was the last time they were out of their cases.

"The SRAM inertial system may have been primitive compared to the ring-laser gyros carried by modern aircraft, but it was a quantum leap in navigation accuracy at the time. (The heart of the system was a pendulum in a liquid-filled chamber.) It took a long time to align on the ground compared to today's systems, which are up to speed in a couple minutes. I don't recall how long ground alignment took, but I believe it was about twenty minutes. However, it could also be aligned in flight, which permitted Alert aircraft to get into the air quickly and align the system on the way to the target area.

"Whichever way it was aligned, it required in-flight position fixes to improve its accuracy en route. It did not use radio aids (or such exotic things as terrain mapping) like modern systems, but got its position updates only from the same navigation radar crosshairs we used for bombing. We were at a turning point in air navigation, and we wanted to make a point with our flight. We planned for celestial navigation at Offutt. However, we considered that the "backup system." Both navigation teams agreed that we would not take a sextant out of its case unless we had to.

"We had a reason for wanting to show what the inertial system could do. We had the SRAM INS, and we knew that much better systems were on the drawing board. (And we weren't even thinking about GPS, which was still kind of gee-whiz science-fiction stuff in Aviation Week to us.) Within the Air Force there was a debate underway about whether or not there was a need to continue training navigators in the art of celestial navigation. Celestial navigation was complex and difficult to train. It was also not very precise, and depended heavily on the skill of the crew. There would be a considerable cost savings by abandoning it, which would greatly shorten the time it took to train new navigators, and eliminate thousands of hours of flight time by eliminating the need to drill through the sky for an hour-and-a-half on training missions to maintain proficiency.

"There was also some question within SAC as to what good it was for a nuclear bomber. We were becoming more and more dependent on missiles as stand-off weapons. The SRAM was already carrying most of our nuclear punch, and the Cruise Missile was on the horizon, so what good would it be to continue on a nuclear strike if we lost the inertial system that they depended on? About all celestial would be good for would be to find our way home if we lost our electronics. So we decided to make the trip without use of celestial in order to showcase the capabilities of the inertial system, and we did.

"I'll concede that we were a bit nervous crossing the Atlantic. The SRAM inertial system really needed a couple hours and several fixes to become accurate, and K. I. Sawyer was close enough to the coast (in aviation terms) that we weren't able to get our systems very tight before we coasted out. Finding ground features identifiable on radar in Canada in March, when everything is still covered with ice and snow, is not easy. But between the two aircraft we had two inertial systems and four experienced navigators, and we compared positions frequently. Our positions matched closely enough that we felt comfortable that we would be in the ballpark when we started looking for our tankers off the Brittany Peninsula. After that we were able to feed the SRAM INS a steady diet of fixes across Europe. By the time we were out of range of land again over the Mediterranean the inertial systems were becoming very accurate and we had no worries about position accuracy for the rest of the mission."

Fuel Planning Changes

Hesser added, "It was obvious to my entire crew that the SAC Mission Planning guys knew what they were doing. We got an education working alongside the SAC staff. They didn't miss a beat. Their thoroughness, and their desire to take our inputs and not only listen, but use them, was especially noteworthy.

"As an example, we requested changes in the planned refuelings. The original plan was for five refuelings of roughly equal size. However, we decided to front-load the refueling. Our concern was that in the back half of the mission fatigue was going to be a problem (which it certainly was). As such, we decided to try to limit the more challenging tasks, such as hanging on to a boom, and requested that the third refueling be changed to a big gulp with a maximum on-load, and smaller refuelings afterwards.

> *"The final plan for the third refueling required seven tankers to deliver both bombers a massive onload of 210,000 lbs. For comparison, a fully loaded Boeing 737-800 weighs only 180,000 lbs. including the aircraft, passengers, and fuel."*

"They did all they could to bring us up-to-date on ICAO flight plans and HF reporting procedures from country-to-country. Everything down to explaining the diplomatic clearances we needed to overfly countries was supplied to us. And even our requests to modify refueling routes and procedures were met with a positive, can-do attitude."

Other items that needed to be addressed were crew rest periods. They had to be adjusted so that the right crewmember got some rest prior to a critical portion of the flight. For the navs downstairs, celestial data was developed in case that last resort form of navigation might be needed if there were problems with the inertial systems onboard.

"It seems like days but it was only hours of mission planning that were spent learning communications tasks and policies around the globe and noting the agencies to contact on our flight plans and charts. For an RN, the more I can put on my chart, the better off I am since I'm looking at it all the time," Hesser said.

The pilot and co-pilot worked with SAC staffers on the Altitude Reservation (ALTRV) forms, and fuel planning was completed including the fuel curves and decision points decided upon in case of the loss of an air refueling or a short load due to weather or mechanical problems.

Hesser, or any other SAC navigator, couldn't help but smile when he described the many different charts and maps required for navigation.

"For a normal training mission in the states, a couple of high level charts glued together and a prepared low level chart were about it. For this one we had thirteen different huge JNC and GNC charts that had to be pared down into a strip chart that was about 35 to 40 feet long. First time the chart, by itself, filled my nav bag...well, almost."

Back from Offutt

No one was supposed to know where a couple of their flight crews had gone for a few days while they were flight planning at SAC Headquarters. So, when they returned, there were various guesses as to what mysterious, top-secret mission they were up to. The two crews involved couldn't even tell their wives.

Hesser continues, "When we got back from mission planning at Offutt we were busy with mission preparation, so I had little time for Lin. In fact, rather than going home I spent the night before the mission on base. Lin and I lived in town, about twenty miles away. (We had arrived at Sawyer shortly after Kincheloe had closed, so we hadn't been able to get base housing.) Normally it was an easy drive, but in March in the Upper Peninsula you don't take anything for granted when it comes to travel. So I didn't see Lin the morning we took off.

According to crewmembers, one of the hardest parts of the pre-mission secrecy was avoiding friends and acquaintances at home to reduce the number of questions they received about their mission. Wing commander, Brigadier General Marion F. Tidwell, gave the crews full authority and all the support he could offer. And he allowed each crew to select their own extra pilot due to the length of the mission.

As for the aircraft, they selected the two airplanes at Sawyer that had the record of the lowest oil consumption "because we knew we could get plenty of gas from the tankers, but you can't change oil in flight," he laughed. "And I think I had half the avionics shop's collection of spare bomb-nav components, just in case."

Ready To Go

The aircraft and spares were all preflighted one day prior to the flight to ensure no last minute glitches would delay the mission launch.

At Offutt, mission planners were putting the final touches on the global weather brief and the flight plan was rechecked and uploaded to the computer. SAC also had the responsibility to gather all the diplomatic clearances and coordinate them both with the crews and the over flight countries involved. All this information was passed on to Sawyer and the primary flight crews there.

The next morning—0825 and one minute later for the second aircraft—the crews launched.

"The first leg of our journey was not rich in radar fixes," said Hesser. "Our route soon took us across the border to eastern Canada. In mid-winter, everything in that part of the world is frozen and covered with snow. The hundreds of little lakes that all looked alike to begin with became almost completely indistinguishable as they froze over and the snow cover blended them with the surrounding area. There was also almost nothing in the way of 'culture' (man-made structures which tended to be good radar reflectors) so we didn't have much to feed our hungry SRAM systems before we coasted out over the North Atlantic.

"But we had enough going for us. We did have two SRAM systems to compare, and four experienced navigators. We compared our positions frequently and found that they matched with a comforting closeness.

"I had picked up the technique of a six-minute DR from a former navigator. Plotting a position every six minutes was more time consuming than the standard fifteen or twenty-minute DR, but that timing made distance computation easy

Crewmembers (in parkas) of the lead B-52 aircraft for the MacKay award winning flight included: kneeling L to R: Maj. William Thurston, AC; Capt. Charles Schencke, Navigator; Capt. Wayne Hesser, RN. Standing L to R: Capt. Cori Kundert, EWO; SSgt Samuel Carmona, Gunner; Capt. Steven Nunn, CP; and Capt. Richard Zimmerman, IP. At far left standing: Col. Robert Rodriguez, 410th BMW DO and far right is Col. Marion Tidwell, Commander, 410th BMW.

(drop the last digit from the ground speed), and it was a highly accurate system. My old nav was uncannily accurate with it. On celestial legs his DR was consistently closer than even our best cel fixes. I was never as good as he was, but with this technique I could beat the stuffings out of a less experienced navigator, and of course blow away the primitive 'counters.'"

Communication Problems

After all the preparation and planning and worrying, the crews agreed that the flight itself was almost anticlimactic. They also agree that if there was one predominant problem, it was communications between the aircraft and SAC headquarters and from the aircraft to other countries they had

**B52H 0042 is the aircraft Hesser and his crew flew on their
Mackay trophy winning non-stop around-the-world flight**

to overfly. Many areas of the world do not use UHF radio at all
but require VHF for air traffic control. The lack of VHF
affected the B-52s, especially in the Mediterranean area. More
on that later.

At times they were unable to receive HF stations for
extended periods. Says pilot Bill Thurston in an article he
authored for Combat Crew Magazine ("The Second Time
Around", June 1980), "We learned to jot down the times as we
crossed each filed point and have estimates for the points
ahead of us because when radio contact was made we could
never be sure which times they would ask for. We also
learned to be flexible since several countries didn't receive our
flight plan and asked us to re-file in the air."

Hesser adds, "There were long periods when we were
either out of communication, or were doing the most indirect
communication imaginable bouncing our HF signals halfway
around the world. I recall one time crossing the Mediterranean
when we were talking with an Air Force station in the Panama
Canal Zone, which was relaying information to SAC

410th Bobardment Wing
B-52 Circumnavigation
12-14 March 1980

Headquarters, where it was presumably being passed to ground controllers.

"Perhaps the biggest communications problem we had was that no one was expecting us. The Air Force (or SAC, or whoever) had coordinated our mission on the diplomatic level, but apparently the word hadn't gotten out to the guy in the radar shack with the radio. We were OK across Europe, but once we left European airspace it seemed that we had nothing but trouble."

Tense Times

"In the eastern Mediterranean we bickered with Athens control, who was telling us we didn't have clearance to cross over to Egyptian airspace. While we were trying to communicate with SAC over the HF to get help, we raised the possibility of orbiting until the clearance issue could be resolved, and then we lost contact. We didn't know it at the time, but though we couldn't communicate with Offutt they were able to hear us, and we almost gave them heart failure when we were asking if we should orbit or turn around. They knew that if we didn't stay on schedule we'd never have enough fuel to continue the mission.

"This was one of the more tense times of the flight. We had lost contact with SAC (which had been intermittent at best), and we were headed to a country that had a good fleet of fighters with a controller telling us that we didn't have clearance. We debated what to do, but Bill Thurston decided to press on and deal with whatever came, which we all applauded.

"We were later told that they got the Egyptian Air Defense Minister out of bed in the middle of the night to make sure no one tried to shoot us down. Apparently that was a job in itself since he was not near our embassy and the telephone system in Cairo at the time was very unreliable.

"Speaking of communications and embassies, we were also told that SAC went to limited communications worldwide so all ears would be available to hear from us if we tried to contact them. We were also told that the Soviets, who knew that something was up, did the same so they could intercept as much of our communication as possible."

EWO Picks Up Targets

We had "hot guns," meaning that we had ammunition loaded in the 20mm. M61 Vulcan Gatling gun in the tail. This was a formidable weapon that could chew up just about anything you pointed it at, but you had to find a fighter pilot accommodating enough to attack you from behind within your cone of fire, and we had little defense against missiles. We weren't counting on being able to fight off any kind of real attack.

As it turned out, we were intercepted entering Egyptian airspace. The gunner reported a couple targets coming up below us that came just close enough for them to make a visual ID. We were reasonably certain they were Egyptian.

After all, we were also going to flagrantly cross the "Line of Death" that Libya's Colonel Gaddafi had drawn across what he believed was his airspace in the eastern Med. If we were going to have trouble during the flight, that's where we were most expecting it." A few years later it would cause armed conflict between Libya and the U.S. The B-52s passed without incident.

"I still remember how striking Egypt looked on radar. It really underlined how the Nile is the lifeblood of the country. There seemed to be cultural development along every inch of its banks, but little or nothing away from its shores".

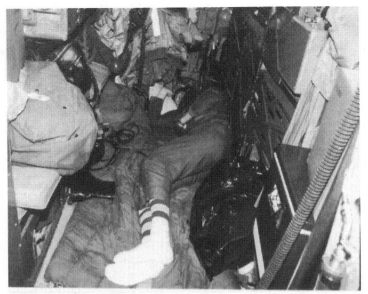

Capt. Zimmerman, the spare pilot (SP) grabs some shut-eye during the 43 hour endurance flight All crewmembers were scheduled for rest as their duties allowed prior to significant inflight activities.

Mission Patch awarded to crew members

Refueling the Beast

Major Thurston: "We had to improvise some formation and air refueling procedures. For example, since no one outside the continental US (CONUS) or Canada would give us an altitude block, we flew nonstandard formation with two-mile, 200-foot separation from the KC-135 tankers. And when our second set of tankers informed us that we could not refuel over the European landmass and only half the on load was complete due to tailwinds, we did the only logical thing. We did a u-turn and headed west to complete the refueling.

"We learned to appreciate KC-135 crews when we arrived at our fourth Air Refueling Control Point (ARCP) in the Indian Ocean with only enough gas to get to Diego Garcia. Our seven tankers arrived on time to offload 210,000 pounds of JP-5 apiece. In fact, every tanker we flew against on this mission was on time; each did everything possible to ensure that we had enough time. Several provided increased offloads without hesitation when we arrived with less than our forecast fuel."

Capt. Wayne Hesser, Lead RN

There is nothing automatic about a B-52 rendezvous with a KC-135 for an in-flight refueling procedure. You basically had two jet aircraft closing head-to-head at 850 mph on offset tracks and someone had to guide both aircraft to the exact position and distance and then direct the tanker to turn directly into the B-52 so it rolled out 2-3 miles (or closer) in front of the B-52 so the bomber could close quickly and have time to get all the fuel it needed to continue the mission.

That someone is the radar-navigator. In this case Capt. Hesser, the lead RN for both crews was responsible to bring not one, but several tankers into position for each air refueling since it took more than one KC-135 to fill up a B-52 when the Buff's tanks were thirsty. Needless to say these refuelings on a secret around-the-world flight to impress the Soviets and the world were critically important. Miss one or don't get enough fuel, and the mission becomes a joke. That didn't happen. Thanks to Capts. Hesser and James McLaughlin, RN in the second aircraft, all five air refuelings went off without a hitch, the tankers were on time and the two RNs guided them into position so that the two beasts ingested all the fuel they needed to continue this vitally important mission.

High Point of the Mission

"The highlight of the mission for all of us," said Maj. Thurston, "was our activity in the Indian Ocean over the USS Nimitz aircraft carrier and the Soviet Navy. We located the lead naval ship using TACAN, and established radio and radar contact. A flight of A-7s was launched to escort us, and we were cleared to descend.

The Nimitz directed us to where the Soviets were, so we were able to find them on radar easily enough and guide our aircraft to fly the RIG around them and photograph them.

Part of the protocol was also not to use the sector scan feature of the radar, which might also be considered a hostile move. However, we also kept this one in our back pocket as a means of jamming their fire control radars in case things did get nasty.

Capt. Hesser continued, "We descended to a few hundred feet off the deck (water) and the A-7s stayed right with us, one aircraft off each wingtip, as we flew our rigging maneuvers over the tailgating Soviet vessels (which always tag along after U.S. carrier groups)."

The rigging maneuver is called that because it is a way to identify a ship by hull features, superstructure, stack position and markings. It's like a fingerprint for each ship at sea.

"It seemed like the whole exercise had something of a festive air to it. We may have been trying to make a deadly serious point about American power in the midst of the Cold War. But on a bright sunny morning in the Arabian Gulf everyone was enjoying themselves. We got close enough to the Soviet ships to see sailors on deck there as well, some with cameras, obviously enjoying the show.

"Before we departed, the Nimitz asked for a flyover. We asked what their highest mast was, and they said 186 feet, so we set our clearance plane for 200 feet and gave them the kind of low pass they probably didn't get every day. (See photo).

A-7 escort off right wing of lead B-52 as it accomplishes rigging maneuver around an unidentified merchant ship so the Soviets could get a good look and understand a message was being sent from the U.S. to the Soviets.

Kashin-class missile destroyer tailing the Nimitz

Photo of USS Nimitz taken from lead B-52 as they began their off-the-deck flyover that the Nimitz requested. The B-52 flew right down the deck of the carrier just to the left of the super-structure on the right side of photo. Cmdr. Pete Vought, one of the carrier's officers later told Capt. Hesser that the flyover was one of the high points of the Nimitz' voyage.

 SSGT Sam Carmona-Gunner

 Capt. Richard Zimmerman-SP

"We could see U.S. sailors watching, photographing, and even waving their arms in a sort of celebration.

After climbing back to altitude from the Nimitz, both B-52s, which burn about 30,000 pounds of fuel an hour at low level, were close to dry tanks. The fourth refueling, south of India, took three tankers each to fill them up to almost full aircraft gross weight of over 400,000 pounds.

Strange Happenings With Singapore Control

One of the strangest things we did because of the diplomatic problems was our flight into Singapore.

SAC had worked out an odd arrangement where we would fly exactly down the border between Malaysian and Indonesian airspace. That way neither side had to admit that they'd granted us over flight.

Unfortunately, as usual, the guy in the radar shack hadn't gotten the world. Singapore Control was irate that we were off the airways, and demanded all sorts of fix and identification information, in between descriptions of all the ways we'd be violated. We obliged them as best we could, and the copilot was still feeding them position information as we flew out of range to the east.

As we headed east toward the Philippines and our fourth refueling with tankers out of Kadena, we changed our flight plan. In part for security, and in part just to cover us in case something went wrong and weren't able to complete the trip, we had filed Anderson AFB, Guam as our destination. But once we were headed out over the Pacific, and we determined that we were good to go, we simply re-filed to K. I. Sawyer.

Many Hours To Go

One might say that, unfortunately, with the bulk of the activity behind them as they "escaped" Singapore Control, they still had about 1/3 of their total flight time left.

Hesser explains. "Fatigue really started to become an issue. No one had slept very well. The H-model has a bunk, but we.

didn't use it as there was more space on the floor of the upper deck to stretch out a little. The bunk was used, as the photo shows, for storage

Not Even Rubber Chicken But Thanks to Keebler!

"Our diet hadn't been that great either. Before the flight a young airman had been dispatched to get us some grub for the flight. We had requested the usual overcooked, greasy, rubbery fried chicken that every flight crewmember is familiar with. Of course, the SAC in-flight kitchen at Sawyer was out of chicken, so the airman went to the commissary to see what he could find.

"He did get some frozen dinners labeled 'chicken in wine sauce,' which turned out to be pretty vile. Only Bill Thurston finished his, and he suffered a sour stomach half the way around the world as a result.

"I don't recall what I ate. I just remember that the navigator and I had this big bag of Keebler chocolate chip cookies, which was empty by the time we landed."

"For me," added Hesser, "the worst time was that last three or four hours. When we coasted into Washington State there was such a comforting feeling of being on home turf again that the adrenalin just stopped flowing and it was a terrible battle to stay awake."

Major Thurston felt that the crew learned a lot about themselves. "Sleep was difficult at best during the first 30 hours due to the activities required to complete the mission. We did try to adhere…to a schedule of meals and drank at least the minimum amount of liquids. Combines with short naps and the (natural) pumping of our adrenaline, this seemed to minimize the fatigue problem associated with the heavy-weight refueling at the 21 and 29 hour points. The last 12 hours, with the major activity behind us, we were each able to get some solid sleep prior to penetration and landing."

A Spy Among The Wives

Since the wives were not told what the secret mission was, they had their own methods to figure it out. As it came time for the husbands to return from wherever they were, they had reached their own conclusions.

Hesser explains. "Though Air Force wives know better than to pry when their husbands are on classified missions, speculation is fair game, and once we were gone Lin and a couple others got together to figure things out. Their ace in the hole was Bea, one of the crew bus drivers who was married to Brent Bunch, the navigator on crew S-21. Bea gave them the crucial bit of information that we had taken extra water jugs. This indicated that we weren't going to land anywhere, so this must be a VERY long flight. Combining that with the fact that we were landing back at Sawyer two days later, they had it pretty much figured out.

Home

As we were inbound, the wives were notified that we were returning and invited out to meet us. They were told that what we had done was classified, so they couldn't tell them about it, but we'd done something really cool and they should be very proud of us. (It takes a good military wife to appreciate such instructions.) It was about three in the morning when we crawled out of our aircraft to greet them, and this was K. I. Sawyer in winter, so the temperature was something south of zero. I think you can see that from the photo.

Respect for the BUFF

In Major Thurston's words: "We came to respect the old buff (sic) a little bit more. Her reliability was proven as the mission had been "OPS Normal" all the way. In 42.5 hours the only significant aircraft maintenance write-up was a malfunction of the AJN-8 heading system on one aircraft. In addition, the reliability of the SRAM for positioning was incredible. The aircraft were always shown to be within two miles of each other. "Reflecting on the mission, the observations we can make are, first, it was done safely. General Leavitt stressed safety above everything else.

L to R, standing: Corrie & Dorothy Kundert; William & Debora Thurston; Martin & Sheila Schencke; Richard & Nancy Zimmerman; Wayne & Linda Hesser. Kneeling: Sam Carmona; Steven Nunn

"Second, worldwide communications and international flight rules are things many of us in B-52 operations are inexperienced in. We need to be aware of the limitations of our equipment as we become more knowledgeable of procedures.

"Finally, we know that the B-52 and SAC aircrews can still hack long endurance missions. They can still fly half way around the world, strike assigned targets, and return home to do it again."

The Big Prize

But the biggest prize was the Mackay Trophy. They flew us and our wives to Washington on one of our base tankers for the presentation. They put us up at the Quality Inn across from the Pentagon, and gave us a day to sightsee, and then presented us the trophy and had a reception where we got to meet more General officers in twenty minutes than we were likely to see the rest of our career (and of course politic for jobs). It was fantastic.

Wayne Hesser's daughter, Angelyn, admiring her Dad's Mackay Trophy on display at the National Air and Space Museum in Washington DC.

Sponsored by the National Aeronautic Association, it is awarded each year by the United States Air Force for the "most meritorious flight of the year" by an Air Force person, persons, or organization.

In 1980 it was awarded to Crews S-21 and S-31 of the 644th Bombardment Squadron, KI Sawyer AFB, Michigan for "executing a nonstop around-the-world mission with the immediate objective of locating and photographing elements of the Soviet Navy operating in the Persian Gulf."

The Mackay trophy has been awarded to aviators such as Eddie Rickenbacker for his 16 air-to-air victories in WWI, Lt. James Doolittle, Lt. Col. Henry "Hap" Arnold, Capt. Chuck Yeager for breaking the sound barrier in the Bell X-1, and the 93d Bombardment Wing for the first non-stop circumnavigation of the globe by three B-52s in 1957.

Capt. Hesser greeted by wife Linda after1980 flight

Maj. Wayne Hesser (USAF, ret.) at his desk recently at American Airlines

Post Mission
"Well, that's about it. It was an exciting adventure, which was an unlikely surprise in a job which can be deadly boring in peacetime. (Do they still say "War is hell, but peace is a pain in the ---"?) I was incredibly lucky to have been in the right place at the right time to have this experience," admits Hesser. "I had my share of bad luck, but I had the Second Time Around flight, so I can't complain. Of course it changed my life in many ways.

"We were later flown down to Carswell AFB in Fort Worth, Texas to be interviewed about the flight. Of course the first thing any SAC troop does when he escapes a northern base is to scout around for a new job. I found a group at Carswell that was doing computer-based training and needed SAC navigators to work on the B-52 OAS/CMC program (Offensive Avionics System/Cruise Missile Carrier).

" It took over a year of bickering with Assignments in Randolph, but I eventually escaped the frozen north to get the Carswell assignment. I won't go through it all here, but that started the chain of events that eventually brought me to my present job managing 737 Ground Training for American Airlines.

"Needless to say it was the high point of my military career. I think it was for most of us, although I lost track of the other crew members. I know several got out before retirement. I heard that Archie McLaughlin, the other Radar Nav, also stayed, but also didn't make Lt. Col. But I can't confirm that. I know Bill Thurston and John Durham both got promoted."

Epilogue

After his Air Force retirement, Wayne went to work for TWA. As soon as his family could fly on TWA under his benefits, he took them to Washington DC. His daughter, Angelyn had only two items on her agenda. She wanted to go see the Constitution…and she wanted to see Daddy's trophy at the Smithsonian.

"That was 20 years ago," Hesser remembers, "but she's never lost the pride she feels about that remarkable flight.

" In July, 2013, Angelyn went to DC again with a boyfriend to visit some his relatives, and of course she dragged him to the Air & Space Museum to see 'her dad's trophy.'

" So, I got another benefit from the flight; I got to be a hero in my daughter's eyes, which is about the best thing a dad can ask for."

B-52 Stratofortress
History, Icon, Legend

"The pride in my Dad's eyes ... that's what I remember. He passed away three years later. But he got to see it—the ceremony—the one where the wing commander awarded me two Distinguished Flying Crosses for heroism in the SAM-filled hostile skies of North Vietnam. My crew led a cell of B-52s into North Vietnam and over Hanoi with broken navigation/bombing equipment. He's been gone many years, and you know what ... it remains my proudest moment. Yes, for what I did in that B-52, but more that he had the opportunity to see those medals pinned on his son. It doesn't get any better than that."

~The Author… A former B-52
Radar-Navigator

The history of one of the finest warplanes ever created—the B-52 Stratofortress—is resplendent with personal stories of loyalty, sacrifice, and service: true reflections on the long and glorious life of a battle- hardened, war-wearied, proud, flop-winged, "take-off nose down," mighty aircraft lovingly nicknamed the Big Ugly Friendly Fellow or "BUFF," and the valiant men and women who have flown her.

It has been said for decades that the last B-52 crew-member has not yet been born. Unbelievably, that same statement is, in all likelihood, still true as this story is published. It's also rumored, tongue-in-cheek, that the Air Force will announce soon that when the B2 stealth bomber is retired, its last crew will be ferried home in a B-52.

It's my airplane. It belongs to the thousands of us who occupied its cockpits and compartments, most of whom would not have given up that challenge as a part of our young lives, for anything. It belongs to heroes like Lt. Cols. (ret.) Jerry Wickline and Myles "Mush" McTernan who are the subjects of our second story, *Last Man Out*. In case you haven't read it yet, Wickline and McTernan were, respectively, the second-to-last and the last man to bail out of the last B-52 shot down during the Vietnam War.

This airplane belongs to Maj. Wayne Hesser (ret.), who navigated it around the world non-stop to an historic rendezvous with the Russian navy and the USS Nimitz, all in record time, and to his fellow crew members who earned the Mackay trophy for their efforts.

And think of a guy like Lt. Col (ret.) Nick Hinch, a B-52 navigator and radar navigator who flew through the combat skies of Vietnam in the black hole downstairs, and then decided he wanted more, so he entered pilot training and came back as both a co-pilot then B-52 aircraft commander, eventually serving as B-52 Squadron Commander at K.I. Sawyer AFB.

Lt. Col. Greg Hennings (ret.) and his former crew can claim part ownership in the big, ugly machine. He's a radar navigator with an unusual Operational Readiness Inspection (ORI) flight that represents countless stories of individual crews who forged successful missions from the scraps of certain failure by performing near-miraculous deeds.

On that ORI mission, the downstairs crew lost their radar with a solid under cast. The pilot unstrapped, and laid himself out between the glare shield and windscreen. The co-pilot rocked the airplane so the prone pilot could peer through almost miniscule breaks in the under cast and call out ground features. Hennings then used that information to dead reckon across the U.S. And, just prior to low level entry, the radar navigator successfully rebuilt a broken radar set. ORI mission complete and successful. And for those who don't know it, a successful ORI mission for a B-52 bomb wing means re-certification as operationally ready. Failure in that regard leads to career-ending reports and lack of promotions for wing commanders on down.

And let's not forget about "Tex" Johnston, Guy Townsend, Bill Allen and George Schairer. George is the guy whose team re-designed the B-52 from a turbo-prop to a jet over a weekend at the Van Cleeve Hotel in Dayton, Ohio in 1948.

The biggest stake in B-52 ownership must be reserved for those crew members who paid the ultimate price over the decades, flying her into dangerous and hostile skies.

In the Beginning

The original specification for the B-52 strategic bomber, issued in November, 1945, called for a six-engine, 240 knot turbo-prop driven, straight winged aircraft with a crew of five turret gunners. Armament proposed was a large number of 20mm cannon and a bomb bay capable of about 10,000 pounds of bombs.

In June, 1946, Boeing's offering was declared the winner. In that same month, Boeing received a contract for a little over $1.5 million to build a full-scale mock-up of the XB-52, complete preliminary engineering and perform testing.

Four months later the Air Force began to express concerns over the enormous size of the aircraft, and, in November, 1946, General Curtis LeMay, then Deputy Chief of Air Staff for Research and Development, expressed the need for a 345 knot aircraft. A number of design changes followed over the next eight months.

By June, 1947 the air force decided that, by the time the aircraft went into production with the additional increased performance changes that had been made, it would be almost obsolete. By late 1947, further design changes and increased performance standards were incorporated into the design.

Almost cancelled in December, 1947, Boeing offered recent innovations such as the capability for aerial refueling and design changes along the lines of a flying wing, and the Secretary of the Air Force ordered Boeing to explore them.

More revisions during 1948 produced a turbo-prop design capable of over 445 knots, a 7000 mile range, 280,000 pound gross weight, carrying the original 10,000 pounds of bombs.

By May of that year Boeing was asked to take a second look at a jet-engined version of the aircraft. At this point there was much concern and debate over the use of this brand new technology to power the aircraft

More debate, additional requirement changes, designs, engineering data, disappointments, and perseverance followed until the fateful month of October, 1948.

After more designs were presented and rejected, the infamous Hotel Van Cleve team of Boeing engineers went to work and a brand new design based on the swept-wing B-47 with eight turbojet engines paired in four pods, a pivotable main landing gear, and aerial refueling technology was presented. This design would meet or exceed all specifications required.

Still, concerns over the range of the aircraft persisted. General LeMay, now Commander of the newly created Strategic Air Command insisted that the Air Force and Boeing proceed and a contract be issued. He also persuaded, cajoled, and demanded that the cockpit be changed from tandem to side-by-side. This change, he claimed, would increase the capabilities of the co-pilot, reduce crew fatigue, and improve cockpit crew co-ordination.

Boeing was awarded a contract for thirteen B-52A aircraft in February, 1951.

On April 15, 1952 at 11:09 a.m., the YB-52 prototype B-52 aircraft with Alvin "Tex" Johnston at the controls began its first takeoff roll from the north end of Boeing Field. As Johnston advanced the eight throttles to full power, the thunderous rumble of the engines caused spectators to cover their ears and cheer at the same time. When the aircraft began its climb, Boeing President Bill Allen yelled, "Pour it on, boy," and waved his arms along with the rest.

That first flight test of the now legendary aircraft lasted 2 hours and 51 minutes. Johnston and his copilot, Lt. Col. Guy Townsend, had just completed, according to Boeing records, the most successful first flight in Boeing history. No one who witnessed that flight, despite its incredible successes, imagined that the plane would still be in active service with the U.S. Air Force over 60 years later.

Anniversaries

April 15th, 2012 marked the 60th anniversary of the B-52. Three years after first-flight, the first B-52 long-range strategic Stratofortress was delivered to the Strategic Air Command for active duty. Only two other aircraft in U.S. military aviation history can mark a 50th anniversary of continuous use with its original primary customer: the USAF C-130 Hercules and the USAF KC-135 Stratotanker. And only the B-52 can claim a 60th continuous-use anniversary.

The B-52H model, 58 of them now assigned to the Air Force Global Strike Command (AFGSC) and 18 assigned to

First flight of Boeing's YB-52 prototype in April, 1952

the Air Force Reserve Command, is the only version left in the active inventory. All other models have been retired. And the H model had its 50th year celebration in 2011. The first B-52H, #60-001, delivered to the 379th Bomb Wing, Wurtsmith AFB, Michigan, in May, 1961.

The B-52 During the Cold War

A total of 744 B-52s were built between 1952 and 1962. Forty-two squadrons at 38 bases operated 650 B-52 Stratofortresses when SAC reached maximum strength in 1963. Originally designed for a nuclear delivery and deterrent role, B-52 crews pulled nuclear alert either on the ground or in the air with the bomber's belly loaded with atomic weapons. The job was simple: if the U.S. was attacked, carry atomic weapons to the Soviet Union and plan on it being a one-way trip. An all-out scenario that included the launch of hundreds of Intercontinental Ballistic Missiles (ICBMs) from underground silos spread across the central U.S. and from submarines hidden and moving beneath the oceans around the world. Fortunately, it never happened.

Members of a Strategic Air Command B-52 combat crew race for their B-52. Half of the SAC bomber and tanker force was on continuous ground alert, ready to be airborne within minutes

Thule Air Base Crash

In 1968, an airborne alert B-52 crashed into the ice near Thule Air Base, Greenland. Before it crashed, the crew released the contents of its bomb bay: four safe nuclear bombs. Though the Air Force spent nine months clearing the crash site, one of the bombs was never recovered.

It is this incident that forced SAC to stop the airborne nuclear alert. Nuclear ground alert continued for 23 years, until 1991, coinciding with the fall of the Soviet Union and the change in nuclear strategy of the U.S. military.

Vietnam and Linebacker II

After the assassination of President John Kennedy in November 1963, Lyndon Johnson moved quickly to up the ante in Vietnam. By June 1965, two dozen or so B-52s dropped conventional 750-pound bombs on concentrations of Viet Cong troops hidden under the dense canopy of a massive, jungle northwest of Saigon. It was the first time the powerful strategic bomber had been used against tactical targets. But the

B-52 missions proved effective and their frequency increased significantly over the following months.

According to General John P. McConnell, then U.S. Air Force Chief of Staff, *"The performance and carrying capacity of this strategic bomber, which make it so suitable for area-bombing with conventional munitions, are not matched by tactical aircraft. If we were to use tactical planes for this task, a number of them would be required to do the job a single B-52 can do."*

By late 1966, the B-52 was used in direct close-in support of ground troops. So many requests arrived from field commanders that a portion of the bombers was designated a quick-reaction force. From mid-1965 to late 1966, B-52s had flown over 750 missions in Vietnam and expended a reign of terror in excess of 260,000,000 pounds of high explosives on the enemy.

General Curtis LeMay was the Commander of Strategic Air Command from 1948 to 1957 when he was appointed Vice Chief of Staff of the U.S. Air Force. LeMay was later named Air Force Chief of Staff. He is credited with building SAC into a modern, efficient, all-jet force composed of 224,000 airmen, 2000 heavy bombers and 800 tanker aircraft. Upon receiving his fourth star in 1951 at age 44, he became the youngest four-star general since Ulysses S. Grant. In 1962 he clashed vociferously with Pres. Kennedy during the Cuban Missile Crisis demanding that we bomb and invade Cuba. His strategy would have been disastrous since the field commanders in Cuba had been given the authority to launch twenty nuclear warheads at American cities and nine tactical nuclear weapons. Millions of Americans could have been killed as well as one hundred million Soviets in a U.S. retaliatory strike.Pres.Kennedy prevailed and his naval blockade worked. After his retirement from the Air Force, LeMay ran as George Wallace's vice-presidential candidate in 1968.He was buried at the Air Force Academy in 1990.

Operation Attleboro

One significant example of this capability occurred north of Saigon, South Vietnam early in the U.S. military involvement in that country. What began as a small-scale, limited-objective combat training exercise for the 196th Light Infantry Brigade (LIB) on September 14, 1966, unexpectedly developed into a widespread, protracted, multi-organizational battle before it ended on November 24, 1966.

It involved 22,000 Allied troops in all, and was the largest U.S. operation of the war to that date. U.S. military spokesmen claimed that the most significant result of Operation Attleboro was the severe blow it struck against the communists' supply system. An enormous Viet Cong base camp, detected during the battle, and seized afterwards by American troops produced a large haul of goods including 25,000 Chinese-made hand grenades, 481 Claymore anti-personnel mines, 80 rocket launchers, 25 machine guns, and significant amount of other weapons, gasoline, tobacco, and clothing.

B-52s, whose program designation then became Arc Light, flew close air support bombing raids on 13 of 14 days, launching from Andersen AFB, Guam to the location of the operation 50 miles northwest of Saigon. A total of 246 sorties dropped 4,500 tons of bombs on enemy troop concentrations, base camps, and supply lines.

Major General F.C. Weyand, Commander during operation Attleboro, said of the heavy bombers' sorties in support of the infantry: *"These B-52 strikes are of incalculable value. They do tremendous damage; they destroy enemy fortifications; and they force Viet Cong field commanders to consider the consequences of massing units preparatory to a large scale attack."*

Between 1965 and mid-1973, B-52s flew more than 126,000 sorties over Southeast Asia, interdicted enemy supply lines in Vietnam, Cambodia and Laos, broke up enemy concentrations surrounding Khe Sanh and An Loc, and struck targets in the heart and lungs of North Vietnam—Hanoi and Haiphong. During this time, 29 B-52s were lost, 17 from enemy SAM 2 missiles and 12 from other causes—most during the Christmas, 1972 11-day LINEBACKER II raids on the North Vietnamese capital and largest port city.

Those strikes on Hanoi and Haiphong are credited with bringing the N. Vietnamese back to the peace table which resulted in the release of hundreds of American POWs from prison camps. (Read more about LINEBACKER II in the first story, Over the Fence.)

The B-52's Expanding Global Mission

From its nuclear cold war capability to its conventional weapons role in Vietnam, the B-52 displayed its versatility. Flying high-level bombing strikes over Hanoi and Haiphong, and forever practicing low-level strike capability at altitudes under 400 feet over the deck back here in the States, confirmed the frontline bomber's value. Since the Vietnam era, the B-52 has participated in all of our nation's conflicts: operation Desert Storm (1991), operation Allied Force—NATO's military operation against Yugoslavia during the Kosovo War (1995), operation Enduring Freedom—Afghanistan (2001), and operation Iraqi Freedom (2003).

The BUFF flew over 1500 sorties during operation Desert Storm and delivered 41 percent of the total weapons dropped by all coalition forces. During operation enduring Freedom in 2001, the B-52 loitered above the battlefields and used precision-guided munitions in a ground support effort. And, in operation Iraqi Freedom, B-52s launched one hundred subsonic cruise missiles to pinpoint accuracy.

Ever-evolving Versions

The B-52B--the first true Stratofortress production model-- was the first model to go operational, in June, 1955. In May 1956, it dropped a live Mark 15 thermonuclear bomb on Bikini

Atoll. Damage to the aircraft occurred when the bomb detonated early, and torqued its fuselage.

The C-model, March 1956, had increased range thanks to larger external tanks. This was the white-belly model, painted to reflect thermal radiation, while the top half of the fuselage retained the natural metal finish.

The B-52D, "tall-tail" workhorse of the Vietnam War, was the first model produced in quantity. After its first flight in May, 1956, 170 D-model aircraft were produced. It entered service in December, 1956 as the first solely dedicated long-range bomber with no reconnaissance pod. They were notable for their black "anti-searchlight" underside and forest camouflage tops.

A B-52 flying at "treetop" level. B-52 crews regularly practice low level navigation, flying skills, and bombing. Note: large shadow of the aircraft on ground.

The E-model first flew in October, 1957. The major difference between the D and the E model was the development of the latter into a low-level bombing platform and the addition of the AN/ASQ-38 Raytheon AN/ASB-4 navigation and bombing radar. This change was necessary due to the improvement of Soviet air defenses.

In May 1958, the B-52F was equipped with new more powerful Pratt & Whitney engines and engine pods that included water injection systems.

The B-52G was the first "wet-wing" BUFF, in which the internal spaces of the wing were utilized for the storage of fuel cells. It had increased range, an improved crew compartment, and a forward gunner station in the main cabin with the rest of the crew. The vertical tail fin was shortened, nose radome lengthened and ailerons eliminated and replaced by spoilers to provide roll control. It became the most-produced B-52 model when the 193rd aircraft rolled out. It entered service in February, 1959. The G-model was also outfitted with under-wing pylons for the AGM28 Hound Dog nuclear cruise missile

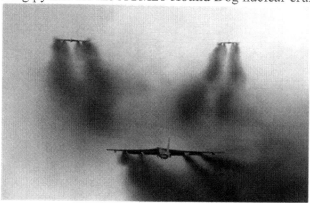

Three B-52 Stratofortress aircraft take off at minimum intervals (MITO) to simulate combat tactics. This is a procedure regularly practiced by B-52 crews.

as well as the AGM-69 SRAM nuclear missile, and ADM-20 Quail decoy missiles.

After the fall of the Soviet Union, the U.S. was forced to eliminate 365 B-52 bombers under the terms of the Strategic Arms Reduction Treaty (START). The aircraft, including all models except the B-52H, were parked at the airplane graveyard at Davis-Monthan Air Force Base, outside Tucson,

Arizona and most were "guillotined" ... a mournful ending for such a faithful servant of thousands of valiant airmen.

The B-52H, first flown in March 1961, was never intended to be produced because the North American XB-70, capable of Mach 3, was meant to replace it.

The turbofan-engined H-model took to the skies with a reinforced low-level-capable structure, aft-mounted GE M61 Vulcan six- barrel Gatling cannon, improved systems all around the aircraft and the capability of carrying the GAM-87 Skybolt ballistic missile under its wings. The current H-model along with the retired G-model is equipped with an electro-optical viewing system in two under-nose "blisters" that house LLTV (low-light-level TV) and FLIR (forward-looking infrared) sensors, used with terrain avoidance radar to provide low-level penetration capability.

Pilots wear night vision goggles to increase safety during night operations and to allow them to more easily clear terrain during low level operations in a darkened environment. The aircraft was also fitted with the IBM AP-101 computer which is the same main computer utilized by the Space Shuttle. In 1989 the aircraft was equipped with GPS.

2007 saw the LITENING targeting pod fitted which gave the aircraft better effectiveness in poor weather conditions to attack ground targets. LITENING also gave the B-52 the capability to carry and use a variety of laser-guided standoff weapons.

How Tuff is the BUFF?

On January 10, 1964, Boeing civilian test pilot Chuck Fisher and his three-man crew lost their tail—the tail of their B-52H Stratofortress that is, at about 14,000 ft. over northern New Mexico's Sangre de Christo Mountains. Their mission was to shake, rattle and roll this big beast at high speed and low altitude to record sensor data on how such a profile affected the B-52's structure. They did their job. The vertical stabilizer blew off. Six hours later and after a lot of engineering on the ground and in the air, Fisher brought his B-52 home, with the coveted data. Airplanes are not supposed to have the capability of flight without a vertical stabilizer.

Chuck Fisher's tail-less B-52

B-1B/B2/B-52 Comparison

The B-52 remains an effective and economical heavy bomber capable of almost any mission thrown at it. It boasts the highest mission capable rate of the three bombers currently in inventory—80 percent—compared to the B-1 at 53 percent and the B-2 at 26 percent. The B1B is twice as expensive to operate in the air as the B-52, but it can cover more territory and move quicker than the BUFF to cover a secondary target. The B-52 is not only cheaper to maintain, but with the development of GPS-guided bombs, it can deliver support to ground forces more cost-effectively. It is the cheapest bomber to operate.

The B-1B and B2 were designed and built to be a high-tech replacement for the BUFF, but the collapse of the Soviet Union and end of the Cold War made that impractical. The anti-aircraft threats to the B-1B and B2 never materialized. This left the B-52 as the most cost-effective way to deliver bombs. The B-1B is now considered the supersonic, low-level, non-nuclear weapon in the long-range bomber arsenal. The B-2, though nuclear capable, numbers only 20 aircraft, and costs $1.01 billion in today's dollars to duplicate.

Top to Bottom: B-52, B-1B, B-2 Stealth Bombers

The Future

"Our B-52s are projected to be in use until 2040. That would make the B-52 almost 80 years old. To give you some perspective, if we look back 80 years, Charles Lindbergh would be making the world's first solo flight of the Atlantic. For over 60 years Air Force bombers have been tasked for both nuclear and conventional operations, but striking the right balance has been and remains a challenge. Since the fall of the Berlin Wall our nuclear-capable bombers have been to war in Desert Storm, Desert Strike, Allied Force, Southern Watch, enduring Freedom, and Iraqi Freedom. They have employed everything from dumb bombs and CBUs, to CALCMs and JDAMS ... Now the B-52 is an amazing aircraft, but we're going to need to manage its sustainment and modernization closely to keep it effective."

~ Lt. Gen. James Kowalski, Commander, Global Strike Command, 18 Feb 2011

There is little question that the B-52 will remain in the U.S. Air Force inventory for over 80 years of active service. In June 2009, Boeing received a $750 million, 10-year contract for sustaining engineering of the B-52. This means continual sustaining, modernizing, and upgrading of the aircraft to meet the war fighting needs of today and the future.

In October, 2010, the Air Force announced an additional $11.9 billion sustainment contract to Boeing for the B-52. This contract gave the B-52 program a "sufficient ceiling" for projects critical to maintaining its mission capability—a second commitment to the future of the aircraft.

Even in the post-cold war period, it is essential that the U.S. preserve the strategic triad that has been the key to deterrence for many decades. Land and sea-based U.S. medium and long-range nuclear missiles serve to increase an adversary's risk of launching an attack against us. And, besides their capability to carry out a broad range of conventional missions, the B-52 and B-2 bombers with stand-off survivability and recall capability are much-valued assets.

Massive Electronics and Armament Upgrade*

CONECT—Combat Network Communications Technology upgrade begun Summer of 2013, will install a digital architecture in the aircraft. It will utilize real-time uplinked data and intelligence in a system of servers, modems, radios, and digital workstations for the crew. They will be able to communicate digitally outside the aircraft and import updated intelligence, threat notifications, targeting, weather data, and transfer it from crewmember to crewmember automatically and digitally.

Since the primary mission of the B52H is long-range and strategic, the aircraft can remain airborne for many hours. Mission planning information is ancient. Radio communication in certain parts of the world can be spotty at

*DOD Buzz, Kris Osborn, July 12, 2013, Military.com

best. (See our previous story). CONECT eliminates that problem and provides the crew with real-time information.

Computer screens in the cockpit will give the pilots a moving map display of terrain as well as graphics showing the flight path. And the new Intelligence Broadcast Receiver and LINK-16 will give them data-linked intelligence and targeting, as well as surveillance and reconnaissance data.

The CONECT program will cost about $1.2 billion and will take several years to install in all of the B-52 aircraft. Funding has been approved for the first 30 aircraft.

The 1760 Internal Weapons Bay Upgrade will allow the aircraft to carry eight of the latest J-series bombs in addition to six on the B-52's under wing pylons. These are the top-of-the-line cutting edge precision-guided JDAM munitions. This IWBU program is expected to cost about $315 million.

The Long Range Strike-Bomber

The next-generation bomber for this country is highly classified but has been designated the LRS-B for "Long Range Strike-Bomber" and is targeted for the mid-2020s.

On 6 January, 2011, Secretary of Defense Robert Gates gave a speech regarding the U.S. defense budget for fiscal year 2012. In that presentation, he announced a major effort to develop a long-range, nuclear-capable bomber, with remote-pilot capability. The LRS-B will be sub-sonic, stealthy and capable of global strategic and tactical strike bombing. It will include modular payload capabilities for intelligence, surveillance, reconnaissance, and electronic attack.

According to one source, global strike Command has made a requirement that the new bomber be capable of carrying a weapon "of similar effect to the existing Massive Ordnance Penetrator," which is a precision-guided 30,000-pound "bunker buster" bomb. The Obama administration set aside $197 million in its 2012 budget request and $6 billion through

2017 to develop the bomber. The Air Force hopes to purchase 80-100 of the $550 million aircraft.

The only other country in development phase of new strategic weaponry comparable to the LRS-B, is Russia. Strange as it may seem, the same timing is set for completion of their aircraft, developed by Tupolev.

There are no "known" new bomber programs with competitive 21st Century technology being pursued by China.

No Stories to Tell

Any history of an aircraft—B-52, B-1, B-2 or any other—is the story of people, of the humans who designed it, created it, maintained it, and flew it. There is no other tale worth telling because without the brave men and women who staked their lives on this glorious hunk of metal, there simply would be no story. And without this wonderful aircraft, the valiant souls would have no stories to tell.

Many crews put their lives on the line to make the BUFF the threat it was and is. Those who lost their lives must be looking down from Heaven in wonderment that the old beast is still one of the most feared weapon systems in the world.

General Characteristics of the B-52H model aircraft:[*]
Primary Function: Heavy bomber
Contractor: Boeing Military Airplane Co.
Power plant: Eight Pratt & Whitney engines TF33-P-3/103 turbofan
Thrust: Each engine up to 17,000 pounds
Wingspan: 185 feet (56.4 meters)
Length: 159 feet, 4 inches (48.5 meters)
Height: 40 feet, 8 inches (12.4 meters)
Weight: Approximately 185,000 pounds (83,250 kilograms)
Maximum Takeoff Weight: 488,000 pounds (219,600 kilograms)
Fuel Capacity: 312,197 pounds (141,610 kilograms)
Payload: 70,000 pounds (31,500 kilograms)
Speed: 650 miles per hour (Mach 0.86)
Range: 8,800 miles (7,652 nautical miles)
Ceiling: 50,000 feet (15,151.5 meters)
Armament: Approximately 70,000 pounds (31,500 kilograms) mixed ordnance -- bombs, mines and missiles. (Modified to carry air-launched cruise missiles)
Crew: Five (aircraft commander, pilot, radar navigator, navigator and electronic warfare officer
Unit Cost: $53.4 million (fiscal 98 constant dollars)
Initial operating capability: May 1961
Inventory: Active force, 85; ANG, 0; Reserve, 9

Acknowledgements

My sincere thanks to the following fellow USAF B-52
crew members who gave generous assistance for this
story:
Maj. (ret.) Ken Brown, radar navigator
Lt. Col. (ret.) Greg Hennings, radar navigator
Maj. (ret.) Wayne Hesser, radar navigator
Lt. Col. (ret.) Nick Hinch, B-52 Squadron Commander,
aircraft commander & radar navigator
Lt. Col. (ret.) Myles McTernan, radar navigator
Lt. Col. (ret,) Jerry Wickline, aircraft commander
Lt. Col. (ret.), Bill Milcarek, aircraft commander

BONUS FEATURE

SAC in Southeast Asia

The Rest of the Story

Based on "The Mighty Eighth"
A Report on SAC in Southeast Asia
Major Wayne Goodson, Director of
Information, Eighth Air Force

SMSgt John Sbrega, Editor

Publication of this story is made possible through the courtesy of the members of the Andersen AFB, Guam Credit Union.

Bullet Shot

No one could have predicted the size a and scope of the build-up that began inauspiciously as the new year, 1972, dawned.

Since 1965, men and hardware of the Strategic Air Command had routinely shuttled to and from the Western Pacific to carry out punishing B-52 strikes against the Viet Cong and North Vietnamese.

Almost every SAC crew member and maintenance specialist had participated in the Southeast Asia action. It had been a long war. Operation Bullet Shot signaled the beginning of the end.

The first Bullet Shot arrivals were experiencing the heat of the tropics before the snows of January and February at their home stations had abated. Most considered this duty as another Arc Light assignment...another 140-179 days away from home and family. Few had an indication that this chapter of the ongoing Arc Light mission was to become one of the most intensive and decisive air campaigns in history.

Intensity

If a beginning date of intense activity can be established, it would be February 14, 1972. On this date B-52s operating from Andersen AFB, Guam and U-Tapao, Thailand, joined in a one-two SAC punch against enemy troop concentrations, supply lines and caches. The one-two punch was to last until the end.

The resumed bombing from Guam, in itself, represented a resolute response to stepped up enemy activity throughout Indochina. It should have been evidence enough that the President's "peace with honor" and "Vietnamization" programs would not be allowed to fail.

It wasn't. North Vietnam misread the tea leaves and made what proved to be a colossal mistake. She went for broke at a time when U.S. involvement in the war was being systematically relinquished to the South Vietnamese.

Protective Umbrella

On March 30, 1972, North Vietnam invaded the South.

Quang Tri province, the northernmost region of South Vietnam, bore the brunt of the massive assault across the DMZ. No less than eleven infantry divisions, some 99,000 men plus four regiments of armor were committed to attack against strategic points throughout the south.

The purpose was the deliver simultaneous knockout blows to ARVN resistance and to U.S. morale at home. They failed on both counts.

And from this point on, Bullet Shot was a misnomer. Instead of limited application of airpower—as a rifle aimed and fired—Bullet Shot became a thundering volley of 500, 750 and 1000 pound bursts of retaliation every hour of every day...100 times and more a day.

The one-two punch of B-52D (foreground) and B-52G in flight.

On April 16th B-52s struck the heartland of North Vietnam with a devastating attack against petroleum tanks, rail lines and

Piers in Haiphong and Thang Hua. It was the first time since 1968 that the North had been bombed. The use of B-52s portended that strategic bombing was no longer ruled out. The enemy took notice.

B-52s strike in support of South Vietnamese troops

With well placed Arc light strikes providing an umbrella of protection, the ARVN forces, by June of 1972 were staging a comeback and experiencing the pride of victory. The impact of B-52 missions in support of ARVN during the Spring offensive is yet to be fully told. Most troop commanders are quick to agree that, without strong U.S. airpower to contend with, North Vietnam would have accomplished most of their objectives with the invasion. By October, 1972, Bullet Shot had become the largest SAC combat operation in the 26-year history of the command. In that same month, peace negotiations resumed. Peace appeared close at hand, but North Vietnam saw a benefit in procrastinating at the peace table to gain battlefield advantage.

The U.S. response, after diplomacy and patience failed, came in the form of Linebacker II, the all-out massive bombing attack against North Vietnam's capital city of Hanoi, and their major port city of Haiphong, December 1972.

Most of that story has already been described in this volume. Here is some of the rest of the story...

Linebacker II-Young Tigers

At 2:51 p.m., December 18, 1972, the first bomb-laden B-52 roared from the Andersen AFB runway. One hour and 43 minutes later, into an exhaust blackened sky, the 87th B-52 followed. These Stratofortresses were to be joined by 40 B-52s from U-Tapao, Thailand.

KC-135 tankers from Eighth Air Force bases throughout the Western Pacific and Southeast Asia also launched. Their role would be to supply pre-strike and post-strike air refueling to all of the 87 Andersen-based B-52s plus vast numbers of Air Force and Navy fighter aircraft. During the next 11 days, the Young Tigers (KC-135s) would fly 1300 sorties refueling every B-52 out of Guam and become the "unsung" heroes of Linebacker II.

People

As outstanding as the flight crews and aircraft performed during Linebacker II, the mission would have been a failure had it not been for thousands of support personnel performing just as well.

Each six-month period saw a 100 per cent turnover of TDY personnel. Thousands of support troops labored under the hot sun of Guam and met all the challenges throughout the Linebacker II activity, which, at times looked like complete chaos and disorganization. But it was anything but that.

Actually, chaos never happened at all. Each man and woman did his or her job...one step at a time...sometimes taking giant steps for time-critical actions, which they almost always were.

Maintenance, munitions, security police, food service, fuels, transportation, communications, aircraft ground crews, bomb loaders, parachute riggers, aircraft fuel technicians—the common denominator was individual troops doing their job well...12 hours a day...7 days a week.

At the height of the build-up, more than 9000 enlisted personnel were TDY to Eighth Air Force, just doing what was asked of them—not glamorous—just back-breaking, knuckle-busting, gut wrenching work. Some didn't get a day off for a month. Men were so exhausted they fell asleep in chairs before they could reach a bed.

Oh, Those Bomb loaders!

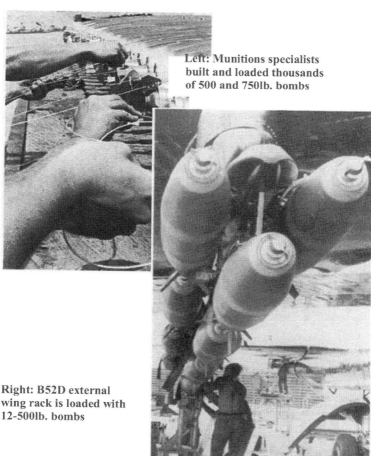

Left: Munitions specialists built and loaded thousands of 500 and 750lb. bombs

Right: B52D external wing rack is loaded with 12-500lb. bombs

It may have been toughest on the bomb loaders. There was no stopping to the bombing or to the bomb loading. Munitions personnel were called upon to load 15,000 tons of bombs in about 250 hours for Linebacker II...and almost impossible assignment...but they did it.

The price was high in pain, puncture and scrape wounds caused by the arming wires that protrude from each weapon and sun exposure and heat exhaustion. Their job was critical. Each weapon had to be built, wired, and loaded perfectly. And that's the way they accomplished this crucially important task-to perfection.

In some cases, in order to get them back to their important work, colonels and staff members walked while bomb loaders rode staff cars to lunch and back.

As was noted by one Chief Master Sergeant, a Munitions Superintendent at U-Tapao, "We witnessed our junior NCO's and airmen put out more concentrated effort than we have ever seen in our Air Force careers—12 to 14 hours a day of solid backbreaking work. The continuous work put out by these men approached the unbelievable stage with never a grip or complaint because they knew what they were doing and why."

**Andersen personnel worship at Tarague Beach
during the 11 days of Christmas, 1972.**

The Andersen flight line during a launch for a massed strike to Hanoi and Haiphong, N. Vietnam...looks like chaos but it's not!

Preview the Prologue of Mrs. President II
Omega Sanction

Moscow, the Kremlin, November 1962

"Do you think for one moment that Lee Oswald was the only one we allowed to return to the United States for a very specific reason?"

"What reason?" Khrushchev's minister of security asked.

"Ah, that you shall know in due time, my friend." Khrushchev held the minister's gaze for a moment with a slight smile that made it clear he knew much the committee member did not know.

"And the others?"

"Ah, yes. The others are, shall we say, a long-term investment, rather like an American, what do you say... Компакт-диск (CD)...ah, yes...certificate of deposit," Khrushchev laughed, "to be invested for the future."

"Kennedy thinks he won the war with his Naval blockade of Cuba. Perhaps the battle, yes? But the war, never. He is too naïve. His own people are against him. I know. I have ears there. We know things, comrade. Eh? What do you think? The world will know. Trust me in this. I may not be around, but all will be taken care of, my friend. Now and many years in the future. Only I know this, but events will take place as they should with or without Nikita Sergeyevich Khrushchev."

"I do not understand."

"Come outside and take a walk with me."

They talked during their stroll through Sokolniki Park near Khrushchev's second residence in Moscow—a habit he relied on for privacy during all his years as premier.

"We told the Americans Lee Oswald was of little use to the KGB--that he worked a menial job in the Minsk radio and TV factory. They never questioned it. Such a minor character. Of what significance could he be to us, the Americans asked me. Ha! They will soon know.

"And, after we brainwashed him and trained him like a little...um, what you say...uh, робот (robot), yes, we sent him back prepared to do what he needs to do. And he will, mark my words, comrade. Do not ask me what. That I cannot say."

"And the others you mentioned, sir?"

"Just as significant as Oswald, and just as indoctrinated should I need them. They are Americans too. They will have American-born children who will not be suspect, raised as good Communists, grow up, and work in the U.S. government. They will work their way into the corridors of Washington D.C., and be of good use to us then, many years, perhaps decades, from now. That is all I can say.

"You will know the truth of Oswald within one year, I think. Then you will also know the truth of the rest, and, comrade, the truth of the brilliance of Nikita Sergeyevich."

Made in the USA
San Bernardino, CA
11 May 2016